How To
WRITE
PLAIN
ENGLISH

M. L. STEIN
DEPARTMENT OF JOURNALISM
CALIFORNIA STATE UNIVERSITY

MONARCH PRESS

Published by
MONARCH PRESS
a division of Simon & Schuster, Inc.
1 West 39th Street
New York, N.Y. 10018

Standard Book Number: 671-18753-8

Printed in the United States of America

CONTENTS

INTRODUCTION

This book is about writing the English language in a clear, understandable way. In my fourteen years as a teacher of writing, I have seen countless students struggle vainly to express their ideas. They often failed because they didn't grasp one principle: plain words and straight sentences are the best means of communicating. Instead, they buried their thoughts in a morass of fancy prose, long, cumbersome sentences and vague descriptions. They didn't come out and say exactly what they meant.

That's what good writing is all about: saying what you mean so it can be understood. Language is a tool. If used properly, it can achieve almost anything you want it to. Wrongly used, it can lead only to obscurity and misunderstanding.

I'm assuming that you know the rules of grammar, syntax and punctuation—or that you have a sense of what is correct. But even this is not a ticket to effective writing. An understanding of the mechanics of English is essential, but it's only a beginning. You must know how to apply this knowledge.

This is what I hope to show you.

M. L. Stein

CHAPTER ONE

What Is Good Writing?

Recent news stories have pointed to a worrisome problem: many young people coming out of elementary and high school can't write plain English. Educators have noted that a number of college applicants who score well on entrance exams turn out dismally poor essays, term papers and other writing assignments after admission. Their communication skills are faulty. They have a weak grasp of grammar, punctuation, syntax and spelling. They can't put their ideas on paper so they come out clearly. Their sentences are long and muddled. They can't come to the point. Students in a leading university turned in term papers with these monstrous sentences:

The native American tended to be prejudiced against, because of their color and savageness.

My opinion about students burning draft cards and insulting the flag should be punished severely.

Everyone has to think of themselves in this doggie world regardless of whether is rich or poor, educated or illiterate, their soul person is to serve societies needs.

It is really to bad when kids learn how to get a grade the easy way like learning how to take a test, or like I always saw when I was in school was teacher pets.

In their want to do good they are extremeily eager to use and support any new method without thoroughly examination the method.

All sorts of reasons have been given for such performances. Some blame it on feeble English instruction in the lower grades. Others attribute it to a switch in philosophy from the traditional three R's to progressive education concepts in which style and grammar are played down. Students are encouraged to "express" themselves creatively rather than be concerned with English fundamentals. High schools are dropping required English courses and permitting students to choose from a wide variety of English-related courses, which may or may not stress writing proficiency. The *Chronicle of Higher Education* noted that the role of college English departments is changing from "introducing students to great literature to introducing a growing number of young adults to literacy—reading, writing, and even to speaking."

Another cause is said to be television. Critics claim that since the advent of TV in the 1940's, both children and adults have turned away from books, magazines and newspapers. Instead of reading, they spend long hours in front of the box, to the detriment of their reading and writing skills.

Whatever the reason, the problem is serious. College and high school teachers have known for some time that scores of students have trouble with the English language. Their weakness not only plagues them through school but hurts them as adults as well. In almost every kind of trade, business or profession, there is a need to communicate—to be understood. The writing of a simple memo or letter requires the ability to put one's thoughts into clear language. Failure in this effort can result in ill feelings, wrong actions, loss of business, unnecessary delay and other undesirable consequences. In diplomacy, wars may erupt because countries cannot get through to each other. In fact, you might say that communication makes the world go around.

Those who contribute most to this communication are usually craftsmen of the highest order. Writing *is* an art. Professional writers are artists in the way they use words. You may never achieve their mastery, but there is no reason why you can't improve your writing. However, first you must know the elements of good writing. They are:

1. Clarity

2. Conciseness

3. Directness

4. Objectivity

5. Simplicity

6. Variety

Let's discuss these one at a time.

Clarity

Good writing is clear writing. It is plain. No one should have trouble figuring out what you're trying to say. A sentence should have immediate impact on any reader of reasonable intelligence. If you want to make a date for lunch, buy a chair, borrow five dollars or have your name taken off a mailing list, make your thought clear. Use words and sentences that can be understood. Don't get tangled up in fancy language or obscure phrases. In the first of these examples, your request might read like this:

Will you please meet me for lunch at 12:30 p.m. Wednesday at the Blue Oyster?

The second note might contain this sentence:

Please send me Danish model chair, No. 45321, advertised in the *Tribune* on September 12. A check for $97.50, which includes sales tax, is enclosed.

And so on. Remember, the purpose of writing is to communicate. Let poets and novelists concern themselves with literary flourishes. Everyday communication has no need for embroidery. And keep in mind that fiction writers do not get published by being hard to understand. They may devote a great deal of thought to a well-turned phrase, but they are usually understood. If you are planning on a professional writing career, the principles just listed are essential.

You can't write clearly by going overboard in impressing your audience with ornate sentences, flowery words or doubtful expressions. When you finish a thought, ask yourself: "Is it clear? Did I say what I meant to say?" If the answer is an honest yes, you're on the way to becoming a good writer.

Conciseness

Some writing is like forgetting to turn off the water faucet. There's more than is needed. The best writing is concise; it says what it has to say and then stops. A frequent fault in high school and college essays is over production. These writers rattle on when they've come to the end of their ideas. Loading extra baggage on a sentence does nothing for the thought and only creates restlessness and boredom in the reader. Here are some sentences that can stand major surgery:

The house was on a wooded hill with trees surrounding it on all sides.

A gourmet is a someone who likes fine foods and wines and is considered an expert in judging the quality of meat and fish dishes as well as desserts whether served in restaurants or the home.

Bicycle riding is becoming quite popular because it's cheap, it doesn't pollute the air and there's a lot of good exercise to be derived from this sport.

Now let's try the sentences this way:

The house on the hill was surrounded by trees.

A gourmet enjoys fine foods and wines and is an expert on their quality.

Bicycle riding is popular because it's cheap, nonpolluting and good exercise.

Directness

Good writers do not mince words. They are direct and to the point. Understanding suffers when true meaning is wrapped in flowery packages. Some people, through a mistaken sense of delicacy, find it hard to describe things as they are. They use such euphemisms as "passed away" for "died" or "a slight indisposition" for "a cold." Words like *obese, discharged, disadvantaged* and *ladies of the evening* are substituted for *fat, fired, poor* and *prostitutes.* The English language needs no such adornments. Plain, direct language is always more effective. It was good enough for Shakespeare, Dickens and Mark Twain. Elegance may be all right for engraved invitations, but not for common, everyday communication. Besides, direct speech and writing cuts down the chances for a misunderstanding that can lead to ill feelings, wrong actions or harmful delays. Direct words and sentences also increase the possibility that your audience will stick with you. When ideas are muffled in a fog of fancy words and phrases, the reader is likely to become impatient. Another problem in communication is failure to get to the crux immediately. This usually means employing forty or fifty words when two or three will do nicely.

A classic example of roundabout, fuzzy language was given by Ron Ziegler when he was press secretary to former president Richard M. Nixon. Asked by a reporter whether a batch of Watergate tape recordings was still intact, Ziegler replied:

> I would feel that most of the conversations that took place in those areas of the White House that did have the recording system would in almost their entirety be in existence but the special prosecutor, the court, and I think, the American people are sufficiently familiar with the recording system to know where the recording devices existed and to know the situation in terms of the recording but I feel, although the process has not been undertaken yet in preparation of the material to abide by the court decision, really, what the answer to that question is.

Mr. Ziegler, of course, was trying to say, "I don't know." For his drawn-out effort, he won the "gobbledygook" category of the "Doublespeak Awards" given by the National Council of Teachers of English.

Resist the urge to pile on unneeded words. If two words will do, why try for ten? Be direct. Say what you have to say and then move on to another idea.

Objectivity

Some of the nation's best writers have been passionate advocates of causes. Upton Sinclair wrote meaningfully and effectively about the evils of the meat packing plants of his day. Tom Paine discoursed eloquently about the cause of liberty in colonial times. Ida Tarbell penned meaningful and effective books on venal oil companies. A modern-day muckraker, Ralph Nader, turned out a blunt, hard-hitting book on unsafe automobiles.

No one would call these writers objective. They had strong ideas on their subjects and expressed them. But in most written communication, advocacy and personal involvement only clutter up meaning. For most purposes, objective writing is more effective. The writer who wants to get an idea across is advised to keep his personal feelings out of letter, memo, essay or article. Instead, he should bring in facts that will support his argument or point of view.

The reader is seldom interested in the personal feelings of the writer. A boss who asks for a memo on a company problem doesn't want the author's own bias to creep into the report. If he desires it, he will ask for it. A complaint to the mayor or city council should concern itself only with the facts. If, for example, garbage collections have been late and overly noisy, the letter should be specific about times and places. A diatribe against city services generally will only confuse the issue and lessen the chances for improvement. Nor will a sermon on punctuality prove effective.

Employment applications also should be free of subjective meandering. The personnel director or whoever does the hiring is interested only in your qualifications for the job. He has neither the time nor the desire to read about your emotional hangups, economic or social opinions or the reasons you chose computer programming over hair dressing as an occupation.

Journalism is an excellent example of objective writing. Some people accuse newspapers and magazines of bias and slanting, but such writing is the exception, not the rule. The great majority of news stories are written in a straight, down-the-middle manner. A tenet of American journalism is that stories be fair and objective, with the reporter's beliefs kept out. The two great wire services,

Associated Press and United Press International, which supply most of the news you read, have objectivity as a required standard. Test this fact yourself by reading a number of news articles for evidence of prejudice. Editorials are something else. A newspaper or magazine is entitled to express its own opinions on the editorial page.

Objective writing also disciplines the mind and sharpens writing skills. If you can present an idea clearly and meaningfully without forcing your own emotions on the reader, you have achieved a breakthrough in communicating. Here is an example of an objective report of a controversial issue by United Press International. Note how the writer's opinions are left out of the story.

CHARLESTON, W. VA. (UPI)—Waving flags and anticommunist placards, 2,000 persons marched through city streets crowded with Christmas shoppers Saturday in a renewed protest against controversial school books.

The demonstration was the first in three weeks by clergy-led parents who believe a new series of texts in Kanawha County schools are obscene, un-American and anti-Christian.

Bundled in heavy clothing and carrying umbrellas in the cold rainy weather, the protesters massed at the Civic Center, a sports arena, and paraded through the downtown area before returning to the arena for a series of speeches.

"This is a national rally against those books," said the Rev. Avis Hill, dressed in buckskin and wearing a coonskin cap, as he led the march.

"I feel that all the carpenters and plumbers should walk off the job and come into the streets," he said. "Shut the valley down, and they'll do what we want them to do."

At the Civic Center, Hill, a fundamentalist preacher, urged the crowd to boycott all area businesses that have not been sympathetic with the protest.

He also asked parents to keep their children from classes beginning Monday. Hill told the protesters that the anti-textbook movement would end only with the removal of the controversial books from the school system. . . .

Some of the books were withdrawn from the school system after the protest started in September, and others were returned after screening by a committee with the provision that no children whose parents objected would have to use them. . . .

The emphasis in the story is on facts and more facts. This should be the aim of most writing. Communication roadblocks occur when the writer attempts to push his own ideas into what should be a fair-minded account. Objective writing is good writing. If you want to pour your heart out in a letter to a friend or lover, that's fine. But for communicating in school, business and journalism, assemble your facts and write them straight.

Simplicity

When it comes to writing, certain people cannot let well enough alone. They'll take a simple subject and make it complicated. Or they'll take a complicated issue and make it even more complicated.

Simplicity is the essence of good writing. Avoid long, complex explanations when simple ones will do. Ideas can often be broken down into their simplest parts for clearer understanding. By simple writing, I do *not* mean *simplistic* writing. Obviously, some topics require more complex treatment than others. But it's also true that much writing is so engulfed in a fog of bloated rhetoric that the reader is left dazed and uncomprehending. "What is he trying to say?" one asks. What, for example, is one expected to make of this sentence:

With respect to their function of teaching the student in the average range, American public elementary and secondary schools have an enormously broad curriculum.

This gem, which was taken from a book on public affairs, can be understood after some pondering, but why should pondering be necessary? The same thing could have been written much more simply and in fewer words. The authors apparently meant that American students are exposed to a broad curriculum. Another tip: stay away from high-sounding phrases like *interpersonal relationships* (the way people get along), *dialogue* (conversation) and *at this point in time* (now). This kind of jargon muddies up communication instead of improving it.

Simplicity, and thus better understanding, can be achieved if you follow these rules:

1. Use familiar, everyday words.

2. Keep most sentences short.

3. Use one idea to a sentence.

4. Depend mostly on the straight declarative sentence, making sure there are a subject and predicate in the right order.

5. Don't write more than you have to.

6. Read over sentences to be sure they make sense.

7. Avoid jargon, that special language of school administrators, businessmen, social workers, law officers and other specialists. Write plain words.

Newsweek and *Time* magazines demonstrate every week that complex subjects can be explained simply and clearly. Here is a *Newsweek* story of an involved matter:

The American Telephone and Telegraph Co. has been the target of government trustbusters for years. As the world's largest corporation, with $67 billion in assets—and a monopoly—AT&T understandably invites close scrutiny. Congressmen, consumer advocates and other critics have complained that AT&T uses its monopoly position to obstruct would-be competitors. In the past, AT&T hasn't had much trouble fighting off such threats to break it up. But last week the giant communication company was faced with its most serious challenge.

In the biggest antitrust suit ever filed, the Justice Department accused the company of conspiring to monopolize the nation's local and long-distance phone service, specialized telecommunications services and the manufacture of much telecommunications equipment. As a remedy, the government called for the breakup of AT&T, whose 22 affiliates service some 110 million phones, or 82 percent of the country's total. Basically, the Justice Department wants AT&T to divest itself of Western Electric Co., its wholly-owned manufacturing arm. It also wants AT&T to split off some or all of its Long Lines Department, which handles 90 percent of all long-distance calls in the U.S., or give up some or all of its operating subsidiaries. The government also warned that it may try to force AT&T to divest itself of Bell Telephone Laboratories, its wholly-owned research arm.

The giant antitrust suit jolted AT&T stock for a day, and brought a quick retort from chairman John D. DeButts. He denied that the company was operating illegally and maintained that AT&T had stayed well within the boundaries of a 1956 consent decree that settled an earlier antitrust suit. By this order, AT&T agreed to limit Western Electric to manufacturing communications equipment. DeButts said he was "astonished" by the suit, considered it "ironic" that it was being pressed in the midst of the war on inflation, argued that the breakup of AT&T would simply increase costs to consumers and vowed to fight the suit to the end. . . .

Simple writing is not writing down to the reader. Let me give you this example from an article I wrote for *Travel* magazine. I was trying to tell tourists what help they can get abroad from American consular offices.

American consular offices in foreign countries are not exactly your home away from home but they offer a wide variety of services for U.S. citizens. It's the wise traveler, however, who knows what kind of help he can and cannot get from these outposts. They do not, the State Department makes clear, attempt to compete with banks, travel agencies, sightseeing services, private detectives and other facilities available locally. And they won't, alas, search for your missing luggage, arrange for driving permits, furnish interpreters or fight your battles with hotel managers. . . .

U.S. consular offices can be found in most major cities abroad and a few that are not so major. In capital cities, they are attached to the embassy. You can usually get their address from your hotel desk, travel agent or taxi driver. They're also listed in the local phone book. It's a good idea to have your passport with you when you are seeking help or information at the consulate.

Check your writing carefully. If you can make it plainer by changing long words to short ones or complex sentences to simpler ones, then do it! The reward will be better communication.

Variety

If variety is the spice of life, it's also one of the main ingredients in good writing. Variety means getting an interesting mix of words, expressions, sentences, phrases and terms. It likewise means using metaphors, similes and emphasis where needed. Variety calls for the avoidance of repetition, hackneyed expressions and overworked truisms. In short, variety means not being dull.

Too many writers feel that their effort will merit attention only if they turn out ponderous sentences, stilted phrases and dreary clichés. They believe this is "playing it safe." Also, they don't employ their imaginations to make writing come alive—to give it color and diversity. What interests the reader is what counts. Any way that you can arouse his curiosity, sense of humor, or even anger is a plus for you. *We write to be read.* You can only turn on a reader by getting him to respond. This is not easy. Thousands of people—perhaps millions—never get beyond the first four or five paragraphs of novels, short stories, articles, nonfiction books and treatises because the writing is numbingly lackluster. Either you grab the reader early, or you don't grab him at all. More about this later.

Sameness in words can defeat a writer's objective. Ask yourself honestly if your vocabulary is broad enough for skilled communication. Professional authors rely on an extensive vocabulary to meet professional goals. When one is writing a hundred-thousand-word novel or even a three-thousand-word magazine article, a ready supply of words is necessary. If you can't think of the right word at the right time, there are reference aids to help you. Among them are *Roget's International Thesaurus, Soule's Dictionary of English Synonyms, A Dictionary of Modern English Usage* by H. W. Fowler and *Webster's New World Dictionary of the American Language.*

Don't repeat the same words over and over again. Let's say that you used the word *quarrel* in your first paragraph. The theme of your article, report or story requires you to convey the same idea several times again. Instead of depending on that word, think of acceptable substitutes such as *disagree, fight, clash, split, feud, squabble* and *rift.* You may be able to draw these from your own word stock, or you can find them in *Roget's,* a book that every writer should have on his desk.

Variety also can be created with sentences. Throw in long ones, short ones and some in between. I prefer the straight, simple sentence, but there's nothing wrong with occasionally switching over to a participial kind of expression if it creates variety while moving the idea along. Take this one, for instance:

Armed only with a tape recorder and plenty of gall, he went to his interview with the crusty historian.

Variety and interest also are enhanced with the use of idiomatic expressions, rather than stiff, formal ones. Trade on the language of the day. Shun archaic, outdated phrases such as *in pursuit of learning, a fallen woman, a foul deed* or *unrequited love.* Not only are these out-of-style, they're moss-ridden from centuries of use.

You really can't be a writer unless you are aware of the world around you. You can boost your vocabulary and improve your powers of expression by reading. Good writers are readers. Read newspapers, magazines and books of different kinds. Popular magazines and paperback books will provide you with examples of "now" styles of writing. Periodicals like *Time, Newsweek, New York, Parade, Family Weekly, Redbook, Harper's, People* and *Ms.* are written by professionals who are "today" oriented, both as to style and content. *Learn from them!* In addition to being up-to-date, men and women who write for a living have mastered the art of clear, interesting exposition. An example is found in this excerpt from a *Parade* magazine article about writer Agatha Christie by Robert G. Deindorfer:

> Agatha Christie today is frail and bent, thinner than she used to be, and walks with a cane. But she dresses with quiet good taste, and in conversation displays a lively mind, a warmth that melts her innate shyness, and a sympathetic outlook toward the younger generation. . . .
>
> Wallingford is where she works best, she says, but in the 54 years she's been an author she has written on trains and steamships, in hotels and resorts, on trips to America, Egypt, France, Austria and even in archeological camps in remote areas of Iraq. . . .
>
> As credible as many of her characters are, she says she hasn't based any of them on real-life people whom she has known intimately or long. However, she does admit to lifting an occasional character from someone she's actually glimpsed for a moment— a beaming, bald-headed man spouting statistics at a nearby table in a restaurant, a birdlike lady peering nervously from a doorway, an elderly Britisher in a wheelchair at a seaside resort. All have been in her books.

It all adds up to lucid readable prose, which should be the goal of every writer.

A number of the points discussed in this chapter will be covered in more detail later on.

Exercises

1. Write an autobiographical sketch, stressing clarity, conciseness and variety. Ask this question of your-

self and someone who knows good writing: Is it readable?

2. Take notes on or record a TV show like "Meet the Press" or "Face the Nation" and write an objective account of it.

3. Clip five news stories you consider models of objectivity and explain why.

4. Come up with plainer substitutes for the following words: *enamored, levitation, multitudinous, derivation, countenance, savant, arbiter, retribution, concomitant, intransigent, immolate, entourage, avaricious, gregarious* and *omnivorous.*

5. Write ten straight declarative sentences on the subject of environmental protection.

CHAPTER TWO

Clear Writing Comes from Clear Thinking

Do you remember how people talk when they're under emotional stress—angry, overjoyed, or excited? The words come rolling out, but often they're unclear, disjointed. A person in a fit of rage cannot collect his thoughts so that they emerge coherently. An individual reporting a crime to the police babbles excitedly but fails to provide essential information, such as where it happened and to whom. Fire alarms are frequently called in by witnesses who neglect to give the location, so hysterical are they.

Such lapses are understandable from persons suffering emotional stress. But they cannot be so easily forgiven in the case of writers who turn out sloppy, hard-to-follow prose under normal working conditions.

You can't write clearly until you begin thinking clearly. Whether you are producing reports, essays, memos, term papers or business letters, you must know what you want to say and then write it clearly and logically. Professional writers *think* before they write. They may sit, staring at their typewriters, for several minutes, sometimes longer. But this usually is not wasted time. They are sorting out ideas in their heads before committing them to print. Even if you have to spend three or four days mulling over your paper, it's well worth it. It's better to stay away from the typewriter or pen than to throw together a bunch of words and sentences that don't make sense.

Here are some suggested guidelines to consider *before* you start writing:

1. Have a firm idea of what you want to say and to whom? What is your purpose?

2. Collect the facts to support your argument or position. Do your homework.

3. Decide on the format you want to use—report, essay, article, etc.

4. Have some idea about length. This, however, can be changed later if necessary.

5. Set aside the time needed for the job.

6. Have the proper reference tools at your elbow.

Now let's consider these steps one by one.

Have a Firm Idea of What You Want to Say and to Whom

A popular myth is that a skilled professional writer can simply sit down at the typewriter and bang away, the words flowing in a steady stream. The truth is something else. Most authors may spend hours and days thinking of their project before they commit a word to paper. And even at the typewriter, they may pause frequently to gather their thoughts, work out the right sentence or develop a smooth transition from one paragraph to another. Newspaper reporters, who are among the fastest writers, often have to stop in midparagraph to think about the story's organization. Wordsmithing is a tough business for professionals and amateurs alike.

Think carefully before you write. Ask yourself what you want to accomplish and what is the best way of going about it. Assume that you're required to write an essay to get into college, qualify for a job or pass a test. You know the purpose. The next thing is to turn your full attention to the subject and how to handle it. This problem is more easily solved if you narrow your focus. Don't bite off more than you can chew. If the topic is rapid transit, stick to it! Don't let your mind and fingers wander into other areas. On the basis of your knowledge and research, plan out your piece. If it helps, do an outline before you write. But put yourself on the right track.

This kind of approach also can be helpful in other kinds of writing. For example, you may have had an experience so amusing, shocking or unusual that you feel it would be of interest to others. Consider first the best way to go about it. Perhaps it will have greater impact if you fictionalize the incident in the third person. If other people were involved, this form would give you greater freedom to develop the event without embarrassing them. On the other hand, a first person, nonfiction account may serve better because the reader would identify with the experience more easily. Your choice would depend on the circumstances.

If time is an important factor, make sure your chronology is in order before you start writing. Are events explained in a logical sequence? This, too, will be the result of planning. Nothing is more confusing than a jumbled set of facts. Writing should be an orderly process. Note how this Associated Press story follows an organized path:

WASHINGTON (AP)—The Food and Drug Administration issued the first federal safety standards Tuesday to protect consumers, students and workers against radiation injuries from lasers.

The devices, which produce concentrated beams of light, are becoming increasingly popular in schools, grocery stores, hospitals and industry.

The FDA said a 1973 survey of lasers found "serious deficiencies in safety practices and in products" in schools and businesses.

Excessive laser radiation can cause severe eye and skin burns.

The standard establishes four classes of lasers, depending upon their power which ranges from a microscopic beam to one several inches in diameter.

Small units used in schools and grocery checkout lines are generally not considered dangerous, the FDA said, but big ones used in industry can burn a hole through heavy steel beams in seconds.

The FDA said it was issuing the laser standard not because there had been large number of injuries, but because the phenomenal growth of the industry potentially exposed more persons to the devices.

About 30,000 lasers now are in use in college and school classrooms for science demonstrations. The 150 laser manufacturers project an 18 per cent growth annually with sales totaling about $310 million this year. The standards go into effect on July 31, 1976. All lasers manufactured after that date must bear labels certifying that they meet the FDA performance standard, and carry safety features and warning labels depending upon the classification.

More powerful lasers must have fail-safe safety interlocks, visible or audible signals when the unit is on, and key-operated switches. Medical lasers used for delicate eye surgery and other procedures must have a way to measure the radiation being emitted.

Laser technology is advancing rapidly.

Low-power units are readily available to hobbyists and are being used in art displays, video replay equipment and alarm systems. More and more supermarkets are switching to check-out systems which use laser beams to read price codes on food and transfer the information to computers.

Moderate and high-power lasers are used in surveying, drilling and cutting metal, fingerprint identification, pollution detection, long-distance communications, weapons systems, navigation, printing, and cutting fabrics in the garment industry.

The FDA's Bureau of Radiological Health said it had reports of only 19 laser injuries during the last five years, most of them involving minor eye damage. But a spokesman said many laser injuries are not reported to the government.

You can achieve the same kind of fluency and organization by mentally shaping the sequence of events before you begin writing. Of course, you won't attain professional quality without practice, but who ever has said that writing is easy?

One way to make it easier is to keep your audience in mind. For whom are you writing? If you're a school administrator communicating with subordinates and teachers, a certain amount of "inside" jargon is permissible. You both speak the same technical language. But if you want to write about the bumblebee for a general readership, forget about high-flown terminology, no matter how much *you* know about the subject. Start with the assumption that your readers know almost nothing about the bee.

In taking examinations, remember that the readers of your answers know a lot about the subject. They can easily spot attempts to pad out an essay on, say, the respective philosophies of Thomas Jefferson and Alexander Hamilton.

Writing for children is an art in itself. Explanations must be made without writing down to them, something they understandably resent. Consider the youngsters' age level, schooling and background. If you're not sure about these factors, talk to the people who can help you—teachers, guidance counselors, curriculum advisers, etc. And there's always the library. Not all children's books are well written, but many of them are. Again, think of your readers before you write. Computer science is a complex matter, but it can be explained to ten-year-olds. It's all in the technique.

Another thing to keep in mind: when you're delivering straight information to any group, keep it plain and un-varnished by your opinions or viewpoint. You are transmitting data about A to B. Don't let anything stand in the way or the message will get messed up. An example is this advice given in *Standard First Aid and Personal Safety*, a book published by the American National Red Cross:

F.   Prevention of sunburn

The most effective sunburn prevention lies in limiting the length of initial exposure at the beginning of warm weather each year, especially for individuals sensitive to the sun. For swimming and sunbathing, the first exposure should not be longer than 15 minutes with gradual increases of from 5 to 10 minutes. On beaches and while boating or fishing, however, both children and adults should avoid long exposures from midmorning until midafternoon. Sunburn may develop following exposure even on a cloudy day.

Persons engaged in outdoor work or sports should wear protective clothing during this critical period, and those with light complexions should cover their hands and faces with suitable ultraviolet-light screening preparations.

The information is right to the point. There is no esoteric language or needless embellishments. If someone wants to know about sunburn, he wants the facts directly. Ponder this the next time you are writing information.

Collect the Facts

Research is an important part of a writer's job. Some find it tedious; others, exhilarating. But it must be done. You can't properly think out a piece until you've collected the data that enables you to see the issue clearly. Facts may be gathered in libraries, archives, newspaper files, home reference books, interviews, etc.

But before you start your search, know what you're looking for! Otherwise, you can waste a lot of time jotting down useless stuff. Unless material bears on your topic, don't bother with it. And make your research as broad as possible. Don't rely on one or two sources. A particular reference book may contain a bibliography that can put you on the trail of further information.

Selection is the name of the game in research, but don't let your preconceived notions limit your quest. Don't pick only those facts which mirror your own notions of the situation or that conform to the conventional wisdom. An objective approach is always more effective in fact-finding. Be curious.

However, some authorities carry more weight than others. A historian with a nationwide reputation should probably be given more attention than the young author of a master's thesis. Also, sources with obvious axes to grind should be viewed with some skepticism, although not necessarily ignored. The essential thing is that you sweep up differing views and opinions to help guide your presentation. This will be less of a problem with pure statistical or historical data. If, for example, you are seeking the nation's gross national product for the years 1963-1968, or the provisions of the Federal Communications Act, there is no need to look beyond a standard reference work such as a recognized encyclopedia or almanac.

Familiarity with your local library is a giant step in researching. Learn about the card catalog, the arrangement of the reference room and the library's other facilities, such as microfilms, recordings and special materials. And don't overlook the librarians as aids in your research. If you have occasion to use a library frequently, get to know the librarians so you can go to them for assistance. They are experts in digging out information. If they don't have it, they usually can tell you where to get it. Many counties and states have cooperating arrangements between local libraries so that if a book isn't available at one, it can be easily ordered from another. By the way, a little apple polishing is sometimes in order in obtaining help from librarians. A writer I know spends a great deal of time in her community library. She always remembers to drop off a gift on appropriate occasions such as Christmas, anniversaries and birthdays. She gets VIP treatment there.

In finding your way around the library, you might start with *The Reader's Guide to Periodical Literature*, a superb source. It lists by author and subject recent and current articles in the nation's major magazines. Let's say you are preparing a report on automobile safety features. The *Guide* may list an article on the subject in *Harper's* three months ago and another in *Reader's Digest* eight months before. *Reader's Guide* volumes go back several years. Larger libraries usually have a file of periodicals, some of which may be checked out. The *Guide* will be discussed in more detail in Chapter Seven.

There comes a time in every writer's life, however, when he or she must interview someone. Not all material can be found in books. Besides, personal comment and opinion can lend weight and authority to your writing. Don't be afraid to seek interviews, even with perfect strangers. Once the ice is broken, you may find that the exchange is not only fruitful but that you are enjoying it! Here are some things to make the interviewing easier and more productive:

1. Always try to make an appointment. The source may not like your dropping in on him, a reaction which could sour the interview.

2. Prepare a few questions in advance to get the interview underway.

3. A little small talk before you get to the nitty-gritty of the meeting helps put the interviewee at ease. You might cause him to freeze up by yanking out a notebook when you walk through the door.

4. Develop a line of questioning that will keep the source on the track. If he strays from the subject, bring him back gently but firmly to the main point. "That's fascinating, Mr. Larabee," you might say, "but can we get back to what you were saying a moment ago about the four-day week?"

5. Keep your cool. Don't argue or debate someone from whom you're trying to extract information. This is contrary to professional standards of interviewing. Submerge your own opinions.

6. But if his replies are vague or ambiguous, it's perfectly fair to ask follow-up questions until you're satisfied.

7. Request that he repeat or spell out technical words and that he explain anything you don't understand. Never walk away from an interview with a hazy picture.

8. Before saying good-by, ask the source to recommend anyone else who might have knowledge of the subject or issue. This could be the most important question you ask.

9. If your notes are handwritten, type them out as soon as you get back to your home or office. They may be hard to decipher three or four weeks later.

10. Check the information against what you received from other sources. Serious discrepancies should be resolved as soon as possible.

11. Decide how you will use the interview results in your report or article. Where does it fit in best? Incidentally, it's always a good idea to take more notes than you'll use. It's much easier to toss out material than to try to get later what you missed. By the time you realize you lack certain specifics, your source may be on a plane for Tokyo.

12. If you quote, quote accurately. Beware of taking remarks out of context. This can distort meaning.

Decide on Your Format

Certain social occasions call for different kinds of dress. You normally don't wear the same attire to an outdoor barbecue as you would to a formal dinner party. It's the same with presenting information. There are various formats for this task and it's important that you select the appropriate one. Such decisions should be based on your audience, how much time you have, the nature of your material, the degree of formality required and past precedents in the matter.

A harried executive who barely has time for lunch will probably not welcome an elaborately bound report that runs twenty-five or thirty pages. A brief memo will suit him fine if it contains the essential facts he needs to know. Personal judgments should be left out unless requested.

On the other hand, a college application essay could well benefit from subjectivity. But even here, the writer should be careful not to clutter it up with irrelevancies. The essay should be neatly written (a typewriter is better) and follow the directives of the admissions office.

If you're attempting to "sell" an idea or plan, a formal brochure or pamphlet may be in order. In making presentations to potential clients, advertising and public relations firms doll up their pitch with handsome binders, expensive art work and other ornaments. The purpose, of course, is to impress the client. It's the same principle used by purveyors of perfume and cosmetics, which come in those swanky boxes. This may be the right technique in some cases.

Pretend that you belong to a group advocating a summer recreation program in your community. Support for the plan must come from the city council. In this instance, a fairly elaborate package would be in order. After you've assembled your data, put it together in a way designed to make the councilmen sit up and take notice. The presentation might be sectioned off into various aspects of the proposal. Other devices such as chapter headings and subheads could help simplify a complex problem. If pictures help, toss them in. But remember, all the window dressing in the world won't help your cause if the hard and compelling facts are not there. Fancy covers and beautiful displays may draw the reader to your offering, but convincing him is another matter.

In term papers, if footnotes are used, stick them at the bottom of the page in which the word or passage is numbered. They should appear only when something needs explanation. A paper can become so bogged down in footnotes that it loses all interest for the reader.

Footnotes can also be placed at the end of your paper, thereby not competing with the content. There also should be a bibliography after the final page. It gives your work authority, indicating to your instructor that you took a serious, scholarly approach to your task. The commonly accepted style for the bibliography goes like this:

Nolen, William A. *A Surgeon's World.* New York: Random House, 1970.

A system begining with the title would take this form:

Secrecy and Publicity. Francis E. Rourke. Baltimore: The Johns Hopkins University Press, 1961.

In the latter form, the articles *the* and *a* never go first even if they are first in the title as in this example:

Mass Media, The. William L. Rivers. New York: Harper & Row, 1964.

A magazine reference is given this way:

Stein, M. L. "West Germany's Adversary Press." *Saturday Review,* May 8, 1971, pp. 47-48.

Make at least one duplicate of every paper or manuscript. Manuscripts are occasionally lost by publishers and high school and college instructors have been known to lose term papers and essays. Carbon paper is quite cheap and copying machines are easily available at low cost. Whatever the price, it beats doing the paper over again.

Have Some Idea about Length

Some newspaper and magazine editors have definite ideas of how long an article should be and will so instruct the writer. More often, though, you must make the decision yourself. Use your common sense about this. If you can tell the story in two hundred words, don't take two thousand. The yield from your research is usually an accurate barometer of how much you should write. If the gleanings are small, don't stretch out a report to make yourself look good. In reality, you'll look bad.

There's an old saying in the newspaper business: when you come to the end, stop. This is sound advice. Journalistic style is direct and to the point. Editors frown on extra words and sentences, penciling them out in a hurry. The noblest punctuation mark in the English language is the period. If more writers used it more often, a lot of communication problems would be solved.

An outline may aid you in keeping a rein on length. Just a simple listing of points to be covered will serve to hold you in bounds. If this doesn't work, there's always editing. All writers must learn to trim their copy—and without mercy!

Write a first draft and then give it a careful appraisal. If you see fat that can be cut out, do it. Is there a paragraph that doesn't belong? Line it out. Have you stuffed in needless detail? Yank it. Do you take too long to come to the point? Maybe your opening needs rewriting so the reader gets the main idea without wading through four or five pages. Objective editing of your work may reduce it by half. If so, the half that remains will be far better than what you started with. Professional writers constantly edit and rewrite. They know that if they don't,

the publisher will do it for them. And that's a lot harder
on the ego. Could you improve on this opening paragraph?

A phenomenon of the past quarter century of social
unrest has been the spectacular rise in America of
what is usually called the underground press. It
reached its peak in the late Sixties and now shows
signs of crisis and decline, leaving some unanswered
questions as the tide of its popularity recedes. They
are questions worth considering in the whole context
of the communications business.

This was written for *Saturday Review* by John Tebbel,
the author of more than sixty books and hundreds of magazine articles. Did you note how the paragraph leaped into
the subject with no lost motion? It's an art Mr. Tebbel
learned through years of practice. Nobody is born a writer.
Style and technique are the payoff of hard work.

Set Aside the Time Needed for the Job

I once asked a group of writers about their work
habits. The variations were broad. Some said they regularly sat down at the typewriter about eight or nine in the
morning and wrote steadily for five or six hours, knocking
off only for lunch. Others admitted they dawdled over
breakfast, read the newspapers and attended to a few chores
before settling down to write about noon or later. Still
others confided they didn't get rolling until late evening
and then labored half the night. One author said he arose
at 4:00 A.M., gulped a cup of coffee and then went into
his study for a solid six hours of work before taking a
break. Afterwards he would wander around town for a
while, and then return home for three more hours at the
machine before calling it a day.

Despite their diverse methods, these men and women
had one obvious thing in common. All had blocked out a
certain portion of the day or night for writing. They knew,
as you probably know, that writing doesn't get done by
thinking or talking about it. There must be a time when
you put the paper in the typewriter and begin hitting the
keys. A blank sheet of paper will still be blank the next
day unless you fill it in.

Work at a pace that fits your schedule and suits your temperament, but work! Tell yourself that your report, article, essay, or term paper, *must* be completed. Then decide where and when you can do it. Plan so that at 5:00 A.M., 3:00 P.M. or 9:00 P.M., you will sit down at your desk and start. Since writing demands great concentration, there should be no distractions from television, radio, children or animals. Some professional writers even pull the plug on their telephones while working. Writing is a lonely chore. It must be if the job is to get done.

If you're involved in a long-term project such as a book, play, thesis, dissertation or lengthy report, try to set up a regular schedule—perhaps three hours a day. A writer who works steadily at his trade develops a kind of rhythm that makes it easier to face that white page every day. After a while, he goes to his typewriter as regularly as he dresses in the morning.

Have the Proper Reference Tools at Your Elbow

As noted earlier, library research is essential. But who wants to run to the library in the middle of a paragraph, just when the writing is going smoothly. Yet, the lack of a single, essential fact can stop you cold. This is why you should have in your home a batch of books for quick and handy reference. It's a collection that can last a lifetime and save you hours of traveling, to say nothing of frustration. Moreover, many of today's encyclopedias, dictionaries, almanacs, etc. are in paperback, making the price palatable. Here's a recommended list:

1. A complete, recognized dictionary. Two of the better ones are *Webster's New World Dictionary of the American Language* and *The Random House College Dictionary.*

2. The *Encyclopaedia Britannica* or an encyclopedia of similar caliber. If this is beyond your budget (secondhand sets are available from bookstores and private parties), by all means buy the *Columbia Encyclopedia,* a one-volume reference that sells in both hard cover and paperback.

3. *Roget's International Thesaurus,* an excellent source for substitute words.

4. *Soule's Dictionary of English Synonyms.*

5. The *World Almanac,* the *Information Please Almanac* or one of the others.

6. H. W. Fowler's *Dictionary of Modern English Usage* and at least one book on grammar.

7. *Bartlett's Familiar Quotations, The Viking Book of Aphorisms* or a similar reference. Sometimes a famous quote or an old saying helps you make your point.

8. A world atlas. There are several, including a first-rate one that is published by *Encyclopaedia Britannica.*

Exercises

1. Assume you're planning a report, term paper or article on consumer action groups. Outline the specifics you would cover.

2. Drop over to your local library. Familiarize yourself throughly with the card catalog, the reference room and the periodical room. If you need help, ask a librarian.

3. Select a magazine article of from thirty-five hundred to five thousand words. See if you can edit out half of it without losing the main elements of the piece. Be sure, also, that the structure is still sound.

4. Take one hour today and devote it *entirely to* writing. Make it two hours tomorrow and three hours the next day. Face the wall, not a window.

5. Check on your reference materials. Do you have enough and the right kind? If not, why not take a trip to the nearest bookstore?

CHAPTER THREE

Words and How to Use Them Effectively

The word *playboy* may be taken as a compliment by one man and as an insult by another. A person may be unemployed because of economic circumstances over which he has no control. Or he may just not like to work. Therefore, the term *unemployed* may not be the right one for both cases. During World War II, the word *dogface* was often used to describe infantrymen. Today, a civilian would probably react negatively to such a description. A wealthy man depicted as "parsimonious" in a biographical sketch may simply be "stingy."

Words, the mainspring of language, represent one of the hardest tasks for the writer. Words convey meaning. Finding the right word is a never-ending challenge. Words must transmit clear, exact meaning. They must get across your idea to the reader. The word may be short or long, one syllable or three, but it must drive home the nail. One of the most unforgivable of writing sins is to confuse the reader with vague, fuzzy language. It's like seeing something through a heavy gauze. Nothing emerges sharply. The writing is out of focus.

To bring your writing into clear, sharp focus, here are some guidelines in the use of words:

1. Lean toward concrete words instead of general ones.

2. Make sure the word is the right one for the idea.

3. Use familiar words.

4. Don't use more words than you need.

5. Use words for color.

Lean toward Concrete Words instead of General Ones

If someone tells you that he saw a "good football game," he isn't telling you much. Good in what sense? Was it well played? Did the favorite team have to come from behind to win? Was there a lot of spectacular passing? Was there a ninety-yard run to a touchdown? Did the third-string quarterback come off the bench with three minutes to play and save the game? In brief, what are the specifics?

Words with exact meaning offer much more to the reader than general ones. *Cottage* is a better term than *house*, *Chevrolet* than *car*, *fifty years* than *a long time*, *orange* than *fruit*, *comedy* than *play*, *Northwestern* than *college* and *two-car collision* than *accident*. Do you see the reason? The first choice is concrete; it creates an instant image for the reader. *Cottage* conjures up a *kind* of house. *Chevrolet* identifies the auto and says something about the likely income of the owner, just as *Lincoln* would. By relying on a precise term, your writing comes alive, providing instant identification. Here are more comparisons. Which use is better?

crime	burglary
sound	cry
garment	shirt
emotional	enraged
magazine	New Yorker
office holder	county clerk
foreigner	Italian
scholar	medievalist

Is there any doubt that the second term is superior? It has a sharper focus. It tells you more. Successful writing depends on furnishing the reader with clear images. Leave no doubts as to what you mean. Generalizations can't always be avoided, but skip around them whenever you can.

Read this passage from *The Spy*, an American classic by James Fenimore Cooper. Note the attention to detail.

A man whose colossal stature manifested the possession of vast strength, entered the room, and removing his cap, he saluted the family with a mildness his appearance did not indicate as belonging to his nature. His dark hair hung around his brow in profusion, though stained with the powder which was worn at that day, and his face was nearly hid in the whiskers by which it was disfigured. Still, the expression of his eye, though piercing, was not bad, and his voice, though deep and powerful, was far from unpleasant.

Cooper painted a vivid portrait. One can almost see the man. The author breathed life into him. Remember this when you want to be descriptive. Pile detail upon detail until your individual, house or landscape takes shape.

Make Sure the Word Is the Right One for the Idea

There probably isn't an author alive who hasn't, at one time or another, agonized over a word—the right word. You must find words that are adequate for the job they must do. A great deal hangs on your subject matter. If you are writing an article about economic conditions, then certain economic terms may be required, such as *recession, slump, buying power, inventories, markup, profit margin, layoff, inflation* and *tax shelter.* If the topic is higher education, such expressions as *semester, admissions, humanities, tenure* and *grade point average* are in order.

Don't reach out for fancy words when plain, ugly ones are demanded. Assume you're writing about slums. Don't call them "poverty-stricken areas." If rats roam tenements, don't refer to a "rodent problem." If junkies and drug pushers blight the neighborhood, don't tag them as "undesirable characters." Use words that fit the circumstances and pinpoint identification.

Writers like Carl Sandburg, Mark Twain, Ernest Hemingway, Thomas Wolfe, Sherwood Anderson and Ring Lardner dug down to bedrock when turning out their novels and short stories. Their words were real and honest. They didn't dish up euphemisms to disguise reality. Don't be afraid of words because they are harsh, brutal or unappetizing. If they're the *right* words, use them. Get on speaking and writing terms with such words as the following:

hick	smash	fat	eat
dirty	grab	grip	fired
cold	punch	hate	belch
sick	sneer	soak	stagger
boil	slam	leer	crazy
grime	greed	yell	dumb
clash	rotten	power	cringe
fail	cut	lurch	shove
stink	rip	crack	bitter
vomit	belly	pus	gamble

Use Familiar Words

Most people feel more comfortable in old, familiar clothes. It's pleasurable to don a worn jacket, a soft pair of shoes or a favorite pair of jeans. It's the same with words. Communication comes easier when the reader is dealing with familiar words. He relates to them. They are what he knows and understands best. The bigger store of such words you have, the more effective writer you'll be. Of course, you should always broaden your vocabulary, but don't inflict unfamiliar words on the reader, especially when they're not called for. If you're describing a picnic, for example, keep in mind that most readers have enjoyed this activity. So write about it in terms that bring instant recollection—even nostalgia. Use words like *cold chicken, grass stains, cold drinks, bright sun, bugs, ants, hamper, peaceful, shady, cleanup* and *full.* Evoke the picture. Make the reader feel that he's there, lounging against a tree, sipping chilled wine from a plastic glass and munching on a drumstick. Don't go out of your way to turn a streamside picnic into an elegant garden party. The words you choose will make the difference.

The problem of picking familiar words becomes simpler if you think of the ones *you* know best. If the word creates the picture in *your* mind, you're on the right track. It's only when writers reach too far for effect that they fail. Some authors like the late John O'Hara are said to have a good ear for dialogue. This means they listen to the way people talk and carry it into their stories. O'Hara, relating an incident in a bar, brings forth a real-life conversation between the bartender and a patron. That's the kind of talk you hear in bars. O'Hara knew what would ring true and what wouldn't. The same can be said for William Faulkner, Bernard Malamud and John Updike. These writers understand their characters and portray them accurately.

Although ordinary, everyday speech lends itself to writing, the relationship can lead one astray. If you listen carefully to the conversation of those around you, you may notice that they often speak in fragmented phrases, seldom making complete sentences. It's hard to write this way and still obey the rules of grammar, syntax and punctuation. The trick is to retain the flavor and meaning of authentic speech and yet meet the requirements of fluid, written English. John Steinbeck did it very well in "The Harness," a short story about a farm woman who has become seriously ill. Note how he captures the essence of the situation in this passage:

> Whenever the word went around among the farms that Emma was sick again, the neighbors waylaid the doctor as he drove by on the river road.
>
> "Oh, I guess she'll be all right," he answered their questions. "She'll have to stay in bed for a couple of weeks."
>
> The good neighbors took cakes to the Randall farm, and they tiptoed into the sickroom, where the little skinny bird of a woman lay in a tremendous walnut bed. She looked at them with her bright little dark eyes.
>
> "Wouldn't you like the curtains up a little, dear?" they asked.
>
> "No, thank you. The light worries my eyes."
>
> "Is there anything we can do for you?"

"No, thank you. Peter does for me very well."

"Just remember, if there's anything you think of ..."

The exchange is real. The words are familiar—the way a farm woman would put it. The stuff of writing is all around you if you're perceptive enough to absorb it. There's more to turning out fiction and nonfiction than merely knowing the right words, but it helps. It's possible to compose a well-constructed sentence that will lack strength because the language is unfamiliar and remote from the reader's experience. Having a character say, "Be sure to lock the door" scores more points than "Make certain that the portal is secured." The latter might have passed when knighthood was in flower, but that's not the way people talk today.

Don't Use More Words Than You Need

Overweight people take steps to correct their condition by dieting or exercising. A lot of writing is overweight and correction follows the same principle of self-discipline. Pinpoint the fat in your writing and remove it—even if it's painful.

Start by eliminating adjectives. Nine-tenths of the adjectives in any paragraph can be removed with no harm done. Indeed, the passage will benefit. Here's a sample of descriptive words that serve no need:

hairy ape	wealthy millionaire
hard cement	dirty cesspool
poor beggar	liquid oil
lethal bullets	dead corpse
fast jetliner	scaly fish
round wheel	unreal mirage
first-year freshman	

The adjectives belabor the obvious. Why use extra words? If you're not careful, you may find yourself writing that "She was making dinner in the kitchen." Where else?

There are other redundancies that frequently crop up. Do you write "9:00 P.M. in the evening" or "white snow was falling"? Phrases like these are quite popular among many people trying to communicate.

Other shortcuts cut down on wordiness without sacrificing meaning. Leave out unneeded words. Instead of "routes that are taken by commuters," substitute "routes taken by commuters." Rather than "violations of the vehicle code," write "vehicle code violations." Newspaper reporters, who must continually concentrate on tightening their copy, automatically reach for the taut combination of words over the roundabout. News stories contain many examples. Compare the phrasing in the two columns below.

At the intersection of Grove and Oak Streets.	At Grove and Oak Streets.
Two cars were in collision.	A two-car collision.
The council voted to adopt an ordinance regulating the activities of door-to-door salesmen.	The council passed an ordinance regulating door-to-door salesmen.
Bogley was indicted on a charge of involuntary manslaughter.	Bogley was indicted for involuntary manslaughter.
A series of lectures on European travel will be offered by the Adult Education Division.	The Adult Education Division will offer a lecture series on European travel.

The last example shows the advantage of the active over the passive. The passive is slower, more cumbersome and less interesting. And it wastes words.

Another waste of words is the useless introduction given to some ideas. Do you see any need for the following sentences to begin as they do?

The long and the short of it is that college tuition is likely to keep rising.

When you get right down to it, western nations should start developing alternate fuel sources.

By my way of thinking, everybody deserves a second chance.

As far as the coach is concerned, the team is ready for Saturday's game.

Repetition also accounts for word wastage. However, repetition is necessary if it makes the thought more understandable, as in this example:

He decided to be a movie critic because he thought the movie was an exciting and changing art form.

On the opposite end of the scale are these needless repetitions:

He was charged with murder *and murder is a serious crime.*

The walk in the fresh air cleared his head *and enabled him to think more clearly.*

When molten metal is immersed in water it produces steam *when it is soaked.*

Since plastic is a tough substance it is hard to bend *it.*

California in the gold rush days was a wild and woolly place *to be living in.*

In each case, the italicized part of the sentence could be sliced away with no loss of meaning. Think of this the next time you edit your manuscript.

Use Words for Color

Color and human interest are what make writing interesting. Some words are drab, while others have zest and sparkle. They give a lift to what otherwise might be a run-of-the mill piece. Words themselves can't make a basically dull subject come radiant, but they can add a little luster. Many of the color words are colloquial or slang. Don't be afraid of them for that reason. Many professional writers use them to good advantage. Here are several words which could enliven your copy:

jazz	blitzed	clipped (over-
con artist	bug (record	charged)
pal	secretly)	bigtime
zapped	saavy	dump (get rid of)
guy	tout	cop
feeler	hip	hood (criminal)
tip off	bust (arrest)	dig (understand)
ambled	ripoff	drag (boring)
tipped (informed)	simpatico	freak (as in pop-
kinky	loot	corn freak)
blackout	sucker	sweetener (some-
		thing extra)

Expressions change. Some of the above may be outdated in a few years. It's up to you to keep abreast of the current idiom—the "in" terms. Dated writing lessens the impact you have on the reader. He may not be a swinger himself in terms of popular usage, but he expects the latest on the printed page. Successful magazine writers in their fifties and sixties make it a point to become familiar with today's language. They know editors have rejection slips for manuscripts that are not in tune with the times.

I'll discuss mood in a later chapter, but it should be obvious to you now that some kinds of writing require a certain formality that leaves little room for swingy terminology. If the chairman of the board asks for a progress report on the sales training program, a flippant or too casual approach would not be in order. By the same token, the report should not be top-heavy with stilted, dead phrases. Even the board chairman deserves better than that.

Exercises

1. Substitute a concrete term for each of these general ones: *ship, city, horse, heavy, smart, building, aircraft, island, wealthy, emotional, dinner, machine, street, weather, educated, fast, dress, tree* and *frequently.*

2. Write a four hundred-word piece on alcoholism, using words most associated with the disease.

3. Pick an article with a subject you know little or nothing about. Change any unfamiliar word to a familiar one.

4. Write an essay on the most exciting event in your life. Then cross out three-fourths of the adjectives.

5. Listen carefully to any conversation between two or more people. As soon after as possible, try to recreate that conversation on paper, sticking as close as you can to the original exchange.

6. Review anything you've written lately. How many possibilities are there for replacing a dull, traditional word with a lively, contemporary one.

CHAPTER FOUR

Writing the Simple Sentence

Writing a straight, clear sentence is essential for effective communication. Meaning and clarity are lost when a writer puts his thoughts into long, complicated sentences. A sentence should be on target—it must say what the writer meant it to say.

Here are five basic rules for better sentences:

1. There should be only one idea to a sentence.
2. The word arrangement, or syntax, must be correct.
3. Use active voice instead of passive.
4. Be specific rather than general.
5. Create interest.

Good writing depends on immediate impact. If the reader has to puzzle over your meaning, you have not written an effective sentence. Your thought should be clear. The following sentences can be quickly understood:

Interest rates for home mortgages will jump from 9 to 10 percent in September.

Sixty million people watched the president speak on television.

Mrs. Henderson wore a plain brown dress and low-heeled shoes.

Newspapers usually put the most important news on the front page.

You must have a valid passport to travel to Europe.

Japanese flower arrangement is beautiful because of its simplicity.

There were nine burglaries in town last month.

Constant airplane travel can be boring and fatiguing.

He is one of three major-league players making over $100,000 a year.

American film producers find it cheaper to make movies in Spain and Yugoslavia than in Hollywood.

Now let's examine the five basic rules for clear sentences.

There Should Be Only One Idea to a Sentence

The period is the most useful punctuation mark in the English language. When you have expressed an idea, stop. Save the next idea for the next sentence. The way to muddle a sentence is by jamming it with two or three different ideas. You get monstrosities like this:

The Board of Education adopted a resolution favoring more state aid and did not take up the matter of tenure for seven teachers who are appealing their termination because of the superintendent's ruling that they did not meet state certification requirements as stated in a recent bill passed by the Legislature.

The sentence is a mess. The reader must juggle two unrelated thoughts instead of concentrating on one. The ideas should be broken up in this manner:

The Board of Education adopted a resolution favoring more state aid. It did not take up the matter of tenure for seven teachers who are appealing their termination. The superintendent has ruled that they did not meet the certification requirements of a new law.

Now the reader can separate the thoughts. Each one makes sense on its own. The "kitchen sink" school of writing is a bad way to convey meaning. Throwing a lot of ideas into a sentence creates confusion. There's no reason why the reader should have to grapple with more than one idea at a time. Clean, straight sentences are more likely when you hold them to twenty-five words or less. This is a rule of thumb, however. The idea should dictate the length. Some sentences may require more than twenty-five words to complete the thought.

The Word Arrangement, or Syntax, Must Be Correct

We all learn early in our schooling that a sentence should contain a subject and predicate. But even with this knowledge, some people manage to turn out clumsy, hard-to-understand writing. Proper sentence structure means that words must be related, as in these examples:

The Coast Guard requires running lights on all vessels.

Sophomores planning on college are asked to meet with Mr. Robbins at 4:00 P.M.

The Long Island Expressway is one of the most heavily traveled roads in the nation.

Prison reform comes more easily when citizens realize that it's in their interest.

American Olympic teams, unlike those of many other countries, are privately financed.

When syntax is out of tune, you may read sentences like these:

She was perched on a high stool with a regal air.
(correct) She was perched regally on a high stool.

The judge warned he would clear the courtroom if there were any demonstrations before he advised the defendant of his rights.
(correct) Before advising the defendant of his rights, the judge warned that he would clear the courtroom if there were any demonstrations.

Walking along Front Street, she saw the huge ocean liner *Queen Elizabeth 2.*
(correct) She saw the huge ocean liner *Queen Elizabeth 2* as she walked along Front Street.

It can be seen from the above sentences that proper syntax means that various parts of the sentence must be in harmony with other parts. Grammarians have come up with various rules covering syntax, but none of them is as effective as common sense. Your own judgment should tell you whether a sentence hangs together in the right way. Such rules as "A subject agrees in number with the verb it governs" are helpful, but most of them are too general to aid the writer with particular problems. After you write a sentence, look at it carefully. Does it make sense? Is the meaning clear? If not, recast it. Even professional authors occasionally rewrite a sentence two or three times until it "reads." If you are in doubt about clarity, read the sentence aloud. How does it sound? If it has a bad ring, you know that something is wrong with it. If you don't trust your own judgment, read it to a friend—a critical one.

Use Active Voice instead of Passive

Certain sentences move, while others lie flat. The difference is important because the first kind excites interest and attention; the second kind invites boredom. In the active voice the subject acts, in contrast to the passive voice in which the subject is acted upon. Active voice sentences are generally more hard-hitting, more direct and stronger. The use of active verbs gives ideas more authority. Compare the following sentences:

(passive) The final touchdown was scored by Ballinger in the last ten seconds of the game.

(active) Ballinger drove over for the final touchdown with ten seconds to play.

(passive) The comedy was performed by the Community Players before five hundred people.

(active) The Community Players staged the comedy before five hundred people.

(passive) An accident in which three teenagers were hurt occurred when a car crossed the dividing stip and struck their auto.

(active) Three teenagers were hurt when their car was struck by another auto that had crossed the dividing strip.

(passive)   The rescue ship was sighted by the ten survivors early in the afternoon.

(active)   The ten survivors sighted the rescue ship in early afternoon.

The passive voice is not to be discarded entirely. Sometimes it's the best form for expressing a certain mood or tone. One example:

As darkness fell, the villagers were seen strolling homeward, talking quietly about the day's events.

The passive voice is also the right one if the receiver of the action is more important than the doer, as in these examples:

Ore is mined in northern Michigan.

Anyone who arrives late will be fined.

But if you read the works of professional writers in books, newspapers and magazines, you'll surely notice that the more robust active voice is used far more frequently than the passive. Newspaper stories are excellent examples of the use of active verbs. A reporter is trained to deliver information with a punch. See this for yourself by leafing through a newspaper for a half hour or so, noting style as well as content.

Be Specific Rather Than General

Fuzzy sentences lack punch. Fuzziness occurs when the writer uses soft, general words instead of hard, specific ones. You communicate more effectively when you describe a man as six feet, four inches tall instead of merely calling him tall. It's much clearer to have the hero drawing $650 from the bank rather than "a large sum of money." "A large sum of money" means different things to different people. A sharecropper might regard $650 as a fortune, while a $150,000-a-year executive would consider it a modest amount. You can't get through to the reader unless your meaning is absolutely plain. Trouble can crop up in any kind of communication—letters, term papers, essays, reports, etc.—when matters are not spelled out. The educator's use of the term *underachiever* is a case in point. This is jargon which means little to the layman. Why not tell where and how a child is doing poorly or failing? *Underachiever* is a cop-out word whose devotees think they're being technical when they're only being obscure.

The best sentences are razor-sharp in their definition, leaving no room for doubt or misunderstanding. A good sentence creates a clear picture as in the following examples:

The men around him were trained engineers and demolition experts who could either build a bridge or blow one up.

Betty Friedan is considered one of the pioneers of the women's liberation movement.

Quint Lewis managed a rock-and-roll band, even though he hated that type of music.

The faded, green wall was peeled and cracked.

In most foreign countries, customs officials are kind to Americans.

Quebec City is for the tourist who wants French charm and flavor without going to France.

Sixty thousand people paid from $4.50 to $8.00 to see the Jets' opening game with the Dallas Cowboys.

A Hindu would rather starve than slaughter a cow for food.

Food prices soared 25 percent in some American cities last year.

Cardiologists claim that heart attacks can be reduced if people eat less, drink less and are less ambitious, less hurried, less hostile and more calm.

He sold his guitar because he needed the money.

The above sentences seem simple enough and they are. Yet, so many people smother their thoughts in a prose so mushy that it barely resembles the English language. Try these sentences for murkiness:

It was a rather nice day.

Jim has lots of personality.

The book is about World War II.

Some jobs are easy to get.

More and more people are using drugs.

When he was in college he went out for sports.

The burglars stole quite a bit from the house.

"But this kind of language is used every day!" you may say. You'd be absolutely right. However, that's no excuse for perpetuating it, especially in writing, where the reader has no opportunity to ask questions that would help him fill in the gaps. The truth is that ordinary conversation is often sloppy and imprecise. A listener frequently nods his head in agreement or understanding when he doesn't actually know what the other person said. Sometimes, the listener doesn't ask for clarification because he doesn't want to seem stupid. Or else he may be so accustomed to this pattern of speech himself that he doesn't give it a second thought. Returning to the above sentences, let's see if they can be made plainer.

It was a warm, sunny day with temperatures in the 70's.

Jim has a pleasant, outgoing personality.

The book is about the Normandy invasion in World War II.

Unskilled jobs are easy to get in industrial areas.

Studies have shown a 20 percent increase over five years ago in the use of tranquilizing drugs.

In college, he played varsity football and baseball.

The burglars stole a color television set, two fur coats, a Nikon camera and $2,500 in cash.

The new sentences are an improvement because they contain more information. The added facts would not be difficult to obtain. The difference between vague and effective writing is often one of detail. The author of effective sentences takes the time and trouble to look up data. He makes sure there is no doubt of what he means. One of the best training grounds for writing is the newspaper business. In this field, reporters *must* have the facts. Their sentences *must* be clear. If they aren't, the editor hands their stories back to them and demands that they plug up the holes. But you don't have to be a reporter to learn the art of exact writing. It merely takes a little more effort on your part, plus a feeling for the English language as a tool for communication—not for abstruseness. Take a look at this example of a fact-crammed paragraph from *Time:*

Statistically, a passenger on a scheduled airline flight in the U.S. has a 99.99992% chance of landing safe and sound. Indeed, Lloyd's of London calculates that a person is 24 times more likely to be killed in a car than in an airplane. Nevertheless, 461 people have died in eight U.S. air crashes so far this year, the worst record of fatalities since 1960. All too often the cause has been a simple mechanical fault or, more disturbing yet, an elementary error committed by a flight crew. As a result, questions are being raised with increasing frequency and urgency about the performance of the Government's bureau charged with the primary responsibility of protecting the flying public: the Federal Aviation Administration.

Create Interest

If variety is the spice of life, it's also the sparkle in a sentence. Good writing need not be dull. Still, dull writing fills the pages of thousands of books, magazines, newspapers, term papers, business and educational reports and official pronouncements. At times, there seems to be a conspiracy to inflict stilted, ponderous sentences on the public. A book on films produced this gem, for example: "The alternation defines the form of the signifier, but not necessarily, as we shall see, that of the significate—which amounts to saying that the relationship between the signifier and significate is not always analogous in the alternating syntagma." The sentence is not only dull, it's stupefying!

Almost any subject can be made interesting by the writer who makes the effort. Among other things, this means finding fresh phrases instead of relying on tired old clichés. It also means varying the style of sentences and not repeating words over and over again. It may involve introducing human interest and color. Or the reader's attention may be attracted by a touch of humor or irony. Any of these devices may be employed without obscuring the meaning of what you're trying to say. Look at this piece of descriptive writing from the book *The Human Brain* by John Pfeiffer:

> The human brain is three pounds of messy substance shut in a dark, warm place—a pinkish-gray mass, moist and rubbery to the touch, about the size of a softball. Shock-absorbing fluid cushions it against bumps, sharp blows and other impacts. It is wrapped in three membranes, including an extra-tough outer envelope, and sets snugly in a crate of bone.
>
> The brain is perched like a flower on the top of a slender stalk which in a six-foot man is not quite a yard long. The top three inches of the stalk, a thick white cable of nerve fibers known as the brainstem, lies entirely within the skull and is partly buried by the bulging halves or hemispheres of the brain. The rest of the long stalk, the spinal cord, is a direct continuation of the cable outside the skull. It runs down through holes in the vertebrae of the spine and ends at the small of the back.

The author reveals an old trick of writers—to relate a technical or difficult subject to familiar objects. Thus, the use of such words as *flower, stalk* and *softball* to sharpen the image for the lay reader.

Here are sentences that make a point of enticing interest:

Tammany, with its back to the wall, was fighting with bare knuckles.

She was barefoot and her hair hung down in spikes over her face.

The short, wiry Troy runs the *Observer* from an old red brick bungalow in Oklahoma City, three blocks from the capitol.

British playwright Tom Stoppard chain smokes ideas like cigarettes and emits the smoke with puffs of mirth.

India's rail network is literally the nation's economic lifeline: more than 60 percent of its goods are transported by trains.

Paul, the bald, drab eavesdropper belongs to the subculture of faceless, joyless professionals who gather at expositions where the latest spying devices are being merchandised.

The way things are shaping up in Congress, millions of people may get substantial tax relief this year despite some of the scariest inflation the U.S. has ever seen.

The above sentences were composed by professionals for news magazines. I'm not suggesting that you can duplicate their skills immediately, but that should be your goal. The prime purpose of writing is to be read. The reader is a fickle animal. If his interest is not piqued at once, he may turn his attention elsewhere. That's why journalism training stresses the importance of the "lead" in the news story. The first paragraph is written to grab the reader and hold him. But don't stop with your first sentence. Make them all as compelling as possible. Exercise your imagination and vocabulary to the utmost. Vary sentences so they're not all long or short or arranged the same way. Notice the mix in this paragraph:

Sporting a luxuriant beard, which caused some persons to suspect him as a spy, St. John roved over Europe during the war years, piling up a series of adventures he later put into two highly readable books. He was in Belgrade when German bombers hit the city and fled just ahead of Nazi troops. With Leigh White of the *New York Post* and Russell Hill, *New York Herald Tribune*, St. John hired a fishing boat to get them across the Adriatic to Greece. They made it, although their pilot was killed by Nazi dive bombers. In Greece, they hopped a troop train which also was sprayed by Nazi aircraft fire. Machine gun bullets found both St. John and White, and the latter was critically wounded. Crawling out of the wrecked train, the three newsmen crouched under a truck as the planes screamed over again and again, dropping bombs and spattering the roadbed with machine gun fire.

No one can expect to be a fluid writer unless he reads widely. The best examples of trenchant writing can be found in books, magazines and newspapers. Writers for these publications have spent years developing their craft. They must please editors before readers and editors themselves are professionals. A professional knows how to write the English language.

A moment ago, I mentioned clichés. You can't always avoid these. Expressions such as "hit the nail on the head," "burning the candle at both ends" and "you can't tell a book by its cover" are old standbys—in some cases going back to Shakespeare. Nevertheless, this is not a reason for being a lazy writer—one who grabs the first bromide that comes to mind without attempting to find a fresh substitute. A writer who relies only on clichés cannot hope to win an audience. Stretch your brain. Find new ways to say things. *Create interest.*

Exercises

1. Break up the following sentences into single-idea sentences:

   a. When millions of people are starving in the world it seems inappropriate to send mining engineers to underdeveloped countries to seek copper deposits when these nations have asked for soil experts and have also requested funds to establish power plants and transportation systems.

   b. After the train was late four days in a row, Bryant decided to commute by car and he also considered moving his business to the suburbs so he could avoid commuting entirely and spend more time with his family, which hadn't had a vacation together in five years.

    c. The high school senior who has sent out col-
lege applications often becomes quite nervous
in late March because he knows the admission
or rejection notices come in April and he begins wondering if he will get into the school of
his choice or get his second or third choices or
be turned down by all of them.

2. Rearrange the syntax in these sentences to make
them more understandable:

    a. Most people have no idea of where it comes
from who use penicillin.

    b. His luggage was in his stateroom for which he
needed three porters.

    c. Ambling along the old trail, the Indian relics
were half buried in the sand when he first
saw them.

3. Put the sentences below into active voice:

    a. The accident in which three people were in-
jured was caused by a collision of two cars.

    b. The hurricane was predicted by the weather
bureau twenty-four hours in advance.

    c. The part was taken by Janice after the girl
who was first given the role was hospitalized
with bronchitis.

4. Make the following sentences more concrete:

    a. The diamond was quite large.

    b. He lived in a house somewhere in the middle
of town.

    c. Afternoon television programs are generally
of one kind.

5. Rewrite these sentences to make them more interesting:

    a. The waitress brought Eric his order.

    b. Dr. Roger Merrit spoke last night to the PTA.

    c. Karate is an interesting sport for different
reasons.

CHAPTER FIVE

Writing The Clear Paragraph

If you can write a clear sentence, composing a paragraph should not be a big problem. You simply string together several of these clear sentences into a lucid, readable paragraph. The sentences should carry the same theme and the finished paragraph should reveal a unified thought. In other words, a series of disconnected sentences may add up to a paragraph in the structural sense but not in terms of understanding. In good writing, sentences flow easily into each other and so do paragraphs. The reader is able to follow the central idea without jarring transitions or irrelevancies. Well-written news stories, magazine articles, short stories and novels take this course.

The principal elements in creating a clear, readable paragraph are as follows:

1. The opening sentence

2. Transition

3. Organization

4. Length

5. Meaning

Now let's review them one at a time.

The Opening Sentence

Composition textbooks speak of the "topic" sentence when discussing paragraphs. This sentence is supposed to establish the topic for the paragraph, and all succeeding sentences are supposed to contribute to the development of this topic.

I see some difficulty with this definition. In my opinion, the first sentence is an introduction to the paragraph. It may or may not announce a topic. The important thing is that it pick up from the preceding paragraph and set the theme for the sentences coming after it. It should also sustain the reader's interest. Study this example:

Union Square in Milford, New Hampshire, population 4,863, is actually an oval. The grassy plot with its faded, gingerbread bandstand splits the tiny business district and serves as a convenient reference point when one gives directions to strangers. "Take a right at the oval and it'll bring you to Route Thirteen."

Milfordites are proud of this landmark, believing that it gives their community a distinctive, New England charm while providing for an orderly flow of traffic. All vehicles must go around the oval to get almost anywhere in the Milford area.

Note how the first sentence of each paragraph plays an introductory role. Observe also that the opening sentence of the second paragraph takes up where the last sentence of the first paragraph left off. This leads to the second element in creating an effective paragraph.

Transition

The mark of the professional writer is an easy transition from sentence to sentence and paragraph to paragraph. Bridges must be created to carry the reader from one idea to another.

There are transitional words to aid you in this process. They include *however, but, despite, meanwhile, therefore, nevertheless* and *notwithstanding.* These devices help swing you from one thought to the next. Warning: if overused, they can induce a deadening formality to your composition.

The best way to ensure smooth transition is to check each sentence and paragraph as you go along. Make sure they're tied together and are not isolated shots. Stick to your theme. Once you go off the track, transition is destroyed. Let's assume you're writing about the women's liberation movement from your own experience. You're telling about the discrimination you suffered in a job interview. If you depart from this incident to recall your recent skiing trip, you will break the reader's train of thought—a train you created. Rambling digressions are one of the surest ways to kill interest.

The best way to achieve harmony and form in writing is to carry an idea from one paragraph to another. Each paragraph should flow naturally from the previous one, bearing its seed. If you're describing the grape-growing process in one paragraph, the next one might point out some of the more desirable areas for grapes. The third may discuss the vinter's labeling procedure and so on. A single thread connects them all. Here is an example in a United Press International news story:

> HAVANA, (UPI)—Two U.S. Senators dined Sunday night with Premier Fidel Castro to discuss whether Cuban-American relations can be improved—just 24 hours after Castro made his harshest speech in months against the United States.
>
> Later, Sens. Jacob K. Javits (R NY) and Claiborne Pell (D-R.I.) said that they believed Castro is interested in working toward better relations with the United States but gave no details. They added, "We might say a normalization of relations."
>
> They made this assessment despite the Cuban's denouncement of President Ford and U.S. policy before thousands in Havana's Revolution Square Saturday night.
>
> Castro refused to answer questions about Cuban-American relations Sunday night on the grounds that he had just given a major television interview. But he did admit that at 47 he can no longer make his curve ball break.
>
> The Cuban leader, dressed in his guerrilla fatigues and paratrooper boots as always, joked with 29 visiting American newsmen for several minutes and posed for pictures before dinner at the Revolution Palace. . . .

And note the transitional flow in this excerpt from *Clipper* magazine:

Can We Save the World's Treasures?

by Beverly Ann Deepe

Flash floods and savage fires have razed whole towns and countrysides. Their destructive whims are familiar and terrible. But now a more pervasive threat eats silently at the world's treasured historic monuments, buildings and shrines. The devastation of air pollution is spreading ominiously over the earth.

The Acropolis, for 25 centuries a memorial of ancient Greece, is crumbling before the corroding agents of 20th century pollution. In Japan, officials consider air pollution "severe" and a threat to the wooden, centuries-old shrines, temples and buildings, especially in the Tokyo and Osaka industrial zones. Even the Taj Mahal, described as closer to "perfection than any other work of man" is being given tests of experimental coatings to protect its marble from the ravages of natural and man-made destruction. In Italy, air pollution consumes the façades of entire cities which are themselves priceless works of art— cities like Venice, Florence and Rome.

Venice is worth a close look. Many of its historic palazzi, churches, architectural treasures—more than 10,000 works of irreplaceable art—are beginning to fall apart, not slowly as before, but almost before one's eyes. Due partially to air pollution, the elegant sculpture on the façade of the San Marco Basilica "crumble at the touch," as one observer noted. A study of the deterioration of Grecian marbles shows that those in Venice are between five and eight times as vulnerable to air pollution as similar stone elsewhere. . . .

Each of the three paragraphs is linked by a common bond: the effect of air pollution on the earth's treasures.

There is no lost motion; the author hews to the subject, developing the theme step-by-step. This is what transition is all about.

The absence of fluid transition results in jerky, hard-to-follow writing. A work of art or architecture has a symmetry that makes it pleasing to the eye. It's the same with writing. Sentences should flow into each other, giving the reader pleasure in being able to easily follow the writer's line of thought. Note how this paragraph maintains a steady rhythm.

Compared with Teddy Roosevelt's free and easy rapport with the press, William Howard Taft's presidency ushered in again the dark ages of White House journalism. He resented and distrusted the newspapers, which, in turn, flailed him hard and often in print. Taft cared so little about his press relations that he didn't even bother to learn the names of the White House correspondents. The main job of his secretary, Fred Carpenter, a mild little man who had been with Taft for years, was to keep people away from the President.

Organization

Organization in writing is like fitting together the pieces in a jigsaw puzzle. The whole picture cannot emerge unless each unit is put into its proper place. Thus, the finished product represents all the pieces put together.

But the paragraph itself must be well organized if the end result is to be a close-knit, polished article, report or story. Every paragraph, regardless of its length, should be centered around a single idea. A new idea calls for a new paragraph. As you write the opening sentence, your thoughts should be on the shape of the paragraph when you've finished it. If you start out with a fact about gold buying, the paragraph should end on that subject. Ask yourself: what is the idea I want to get across in *this* paragraph? Then organize your sentences around that idea. Standing by itself, the paragraph should make sense. Look at this one from a book about war correspondents:

Censorship was in full force for correspondents on all fronts. The delay in dispatches from London climbed from an hour to five hours a month after hostilities started. Italy, Poland and Germany also subjected stories by neutral reporters to a rigid screening, which meant they were sometimes not sent at all. *The Herald Tribune* was forced to abandon its direct telephone line from London to New York and had to rely on regular cable.

The paragraph is organized around the idea of censorship. Each sentence contributes to this subject, developing it in detail. Your subject might be correspondence schools. The first sentence could be "Correspondence schools are proliferating around the nation." The rest of the paragraph could go like this:

New York leads the nation with 187. Next are Illinois with 112 and Ohio with 98. Many are well-established institutions such as the La Salle Extension University in Chicago but a growing number have appeared in the last three years as thousands of Americans decided that studying at home was cheaper and easier.

Okay, that takes care of the dimensions of the topic. The next paragraph could focus on the problem created by the schools. This would be the key to organizing it. How about this?

As the schools have grown in popularity, so have the complaints. Consumer fraud departments in several states have acted against the fly-by-night schools after students charged they were ripped off by false promises, poor instruction and hidden costs. In some cases, the "school" consisted of a post office box or a one-room operation in a downtown office building.

The whole story should unfold in this manner with each paragraph organized around a central theme so that it blends in with the one following it. It may be harder than it sounds, but writing requires constant application. You've got to work at it. Rewrite a paragraph five times or more to get it right. This may seem like a chore—and it is. But writers learn by writing. Distrust any suggestion that there might be shortcuts.

Length

Not much time need be spent on this element. Length depends on what you have to say. A three-sentence paragraph can be just as compelling as a ten-sentence one—maybe more so. When you've exhausted the idea for the paragraph, stop and go on to the next one. Don't drag it out. Remember, paragraphs were invented to provide a break for the reader, who otherwise might be consumed by boredom and/or frustration in struggling through a ninety-six sentence one. A short paragraph gives him time to catch his breath.

On the other hand, a long paragraph may be more suitable. If you have enough to say and you're building momentum, keep going until you've said it. Chopping off the paragraph before its natural end may cause the loss of the mood, excitement or suspense you're trying to create. It could also result in a hobbled, disconnected structure.

You may have noticed that magazine paragraphs are generally longer than those in newspaper stories. This is based on the assumption that the newspaper reader is a hurried individual who gulps down the news as quickly as possible and is somewhat repelled by the solid gray matter on the page. Besides, news is usually edited and condensed before it appears in print. Brief graphs are aids in telling the story quickly.

The magazine reader has more time. Also, he has paid more for the product and wants to get his money's worth. The writer, however, is thinking more about the fact that he must hold the reader's attention for a three thousand-to-five-thousand-word article. So, if he can rivet the reader's eye to a long but fascinating first paragraph, he may hook him all the way. And, since there is more to tell in a magazine article, the author can afford to invest in longer paragraphs—if they sustain interest. This also holds true for books.

My advice is that if you are preparing a report for dynamic, time-conscious people, rely on short paragraphs. Stick to the point and eliminate wordiness. Ditto for slow thinkers and readers.

The length of school papers often depends on the peculiarities of the instructor. A teacher searching only for content may not care about style at all. But as one who has waded through hundreds of term papers and other assignments, I take my hat off to the student who serves up crisp, short and well-documented paragraphs—neatly typed. A long, winding paragraph is more apt to turn off the instructor than a short, tight one.

Meaning

Have you ever read a paragraph that left you puzzled as to its meaning? "What was the writer trying to say?" you asked. Examine each of your paragraphs for meaning. Is there a clearly understandable idea? Grammatical precision does not always add up to meaning. Words and sentences can be strung neatly together without adding to one's store of knowledge.

Here are some questions to ask yourself:

1. Does your paragraph say what you wanted it to say?

2. Can an idea be extracted from it?

3. Is it stated in terms your reader can understand?

4. Are there any questions left unanswered? (Unless you plan to cover them in subsequent paragraphs.)

5. Is there any blurring that could be sharpened by a rewrite of the paragraph?

Style is important, but don't write for the sake of style alone. A well-turned phrase is a delight only when there is meaning behind it. When Patrick Henry said, "Give me liberty or give me death," everyone knew what he was talking about. Similarly, when Voltaire declared, "I may not agree with what you say but I shall defend to the death your right to say it," the issue was clear.

On occasion, meaning can be supported by quoting authority. If you're writing about speech therapy clinics, comments from a clinic director or noted therapist can crystalize the meaning of your paragraph. Comparisons and allusions also help. Reporting that a forest fire destroyed three thousand acres of timber will take on more meaning if you point out that the loss could have supplied enough lumber for ten thousand homes.

Illustration is another way to add meaning and dimension. Let's assume you're hammering out a paragraph about automobile safety features. Going from the general to the specific, you might note that the retractable bumper on late-model cars has reduced insurance rates as well as cut repair costs. To illustrate your contention that college students today are older than a generation ago, you could cite statistics from four or five universities around the nation, showing that the average age of their undergraduates is twenty-three.

Judge these paragraphs for meaning:

Among the many substantial public companies in which family control has made it possible for sons to follow in their fathers' footsteps are A. O. Smith Corporation, Joseph Schlitz Brewing Company, Campbell Soup, Jonathan Logan, H. J. Heinz, Anheuser-Busch, Douglas Aircraft, General Tire, Hotel Corporation of America, Sheraton Hotels, Howard Johnson's, Johnson's Wax, International Business Machines and Radio Corporation of America.

—David Finn
The Corporate Oligarch

In downtown Philadelphia there is a cluttered little store where you can purchase just about anything at incredibly low prices. The store is perhaps 15 feet wide and 40 feet deep and stacked from floor to ceiling with goodies of every description. Outside, except when it's raining, sits a lawn chair or two and, when the little store is empty of customers, the proprietor sits there too, sometimes in his Hanes undershirt, following the street action. Although to the casual passer-by, he hardly looks the part, this small-businessman sitting proudly in front of his modest general merchandise store in his sweaty Hanes undershirt, is also an important East Coast underworld figure. He is a fence.

—*New York Times Book Review*

At a time when Yellowstone could record but a scant five hundred visitors, Yosemite Valley was already a thriving tourist resort. There is doubt that any scenic locality ever enjoyed such a quick publicity and growth. Within a year from the day when the Mariposa *Gazette* published the account of the Hutchings tourist party's expedition into the area, a camp for travelers had been built on the south fork of the Merced, and trails for saddle parties were being pushed toward the valley floor. The Hutchings account was reproduced all over the country and found its way to Europe. On to Yosemite!

—Freeman Tilden
The National Parks

When it comes to creating new specialty circles, one of the most successful publishing houses has been a firm of educational magazines whose output, or at least several of its magazines, is known in millions of American homes. Scholastic Magazines has not only a dozen periodicals but also publishes a library of supplemental readers and popular books for young people. Millions of school kids have reached over the years for *Junior* or *Senior Scholastic, World Week, Co-ed* or *Young Miss* among others, some of which had outlasted their usefulness in the early 1970's and were discontinued. Their teachers also have been provided with suitable periodicals. This output is part of a large circle identified as the juvenile magazines, also populated by such newsstand fare as *Seventeen, 16, Teen Screen, Teens* and *Ingenue*.

Roland E. Wolseley
The Changing Magazine

Each of these paragraphs has one thing in common: clear meaning. They are informative, factual and amply illustrated. They can stand by themselves.

Now that we have the sentences and paragraphs out of the way, we can learn how they're arranged for the total composition.

Exercises

1. Write a vibrant opening sentence for a paragraph on the most interesting experience in your life.

2. Write four opening paragraphs on the structure of your local government. There must be smooth transition from paragraph to paragraph.

3. Choose from current newspapers or magazines three paragraphs that you consider well organized. Be prepared to defend your choices.

4. Write two paragraphs on either off-shore oil drilling or strip mining, citing authority, facts and figures.

5. Find in books or magazines two paragraphs in which you think the meaning is very clear and two whose meaning you consider hard to grasp.

CHAPTER SIX

Writing the Essay

Since essays take various forms, it's impractical to lay down a blanket set of guidelines. Of course, the principles of good writing apply to all types of essays. Hopefully, this chapter will steer you away from some of the pitfalls of essay writing—and there are many. As a form of personal expression, the essay has an honorable history, despite the abuses it has suffered. Let's try to maintain the tradition.

The following kinds of essays will be reviewed:

1. Personal experience
2. Opinion
3. Argumentative
4. Critical
5. General

The Essay of Personal Experience

Before you put a word on paper, ask yourself: "Is my experience worth writing about?" If you're simply seeking a means of self-expression, an outlet for your emotions, that's one thing. But if your goal is to interest the reader in your experience, that's another. Most of us lead ordinary lives, with one or two exceptions worth noting. The worst mistake you can make is to present a perfectly commonplace occurrence as a vivid, strange, unusual or humorous experience. The reader won't buy it and shouldn't.

Professional writers (and some not so professional) have sold their personal experiences to such magazines as *Reader's Digest, True, Parade* and others. But look at the experiences. *Reader's Digest*, for example, ran one entitled

"I Died at 10:52 A.M." The author's heart stopped beating for twenty-three minutes after he collapsed in his car. His life was saved by prompt emergency treatment. Medically speaking, he had been dead.

Other persons have written about their first experience with a mugger, being lost in a remote wilderness, shooting dangerous rapids in a canoe, surviving an air crash, being arrested in a foreign country, meeting a famous figure and searching for diamonds in South American jungles. These are the sorts of adventures that don't happen every day.

Not all personal experiences have to be that dramatic to merit publication or the favorable attention of a school instructor. Poignant essays have been composed on the care and feeding of a stray cat, an immigrant's adjustment to America and a couple's efforts to adopt a child. It all depends on how well the story is told and the inherent elements of pathos, comedy, tragedy, coincidence, etc. Jack Smith, a *Los Angeles Times* columnist, writes about familiar human foibles (usually his own), domestic frustrations and the male passion for Sunday football on television. But he does it with style and wit, giving seemingly trivial incidents a glow they would not otherwise have. Here's his observation on women and football:

> There seems to have been some truth in my thought that to make football fans out of women you would have had to get them when they were little girls. An understanding of football evidently isn't something a woman can acquire after marriage simply to accommodate a husband.

The opening sentence of the personal essay should instantly command notice. A beginning such as "One Saturday morning I decided to clean out the attic" is not likely to leave the reader panting for more. So how about, "While cleaning the attic one Saturday morning, I found an old photo which nearly destroyed my marriage."

I offer these further samples of personal essay starters:

I didn't believe in miracles until I found $50,000 in my glove compartment one morning.

How do you get to be the first girl to cover a football game from the pressbox?

The highway seemed a good place to make an emergency landing until I saw the truck labeled "High Explosives."

Having a boa constrictor as a pet was not my idea— or the snake's.

There was a little mixup at the Shubert Theatre last week. The President of the United States and the First Lady were sitting in our seats.

I didn't pay much attention to the hole in our backyard until the day it swallowed the barbecue set, a bicycle and two lawn chairs.

Use of the first person is inevitable in a personal experience essay, but try and keep it to a minimum. Too many *I*'s make it seem like too much of an ego trip. It's possible to write about events in your life without frequent reference to yourself. Here's an example:

Nobody in our town minded that Al Jenkins had been to prison. He went about his business and caused no trouble. I first met him at the library check-out line. He was loaded down with about eight books compared to the one in my hand. Gallantly, he motioned me to go ahead of him. We did an Alphonse and Gaston act for a minute or so as those behind us mumbled impatiently.

And remember that it's all right to evoke emotion but don't let it drip all over the page. An essay loses its effect when the writer becomes too saccharine. Let the story tell itself rather than figuratively grab the reader by the lapels and tell him how sad, pitiful or comic your experience was. If the material is there, the emotion can be created without using artificial devices.

The Opinion Essay

Our opinions are one of the cheapest commodities on the market. Unless one is a recognized expert or authority, his opinion is rarely, if ever, sought. Still, people insist on expressing their views in letters to the editor, notes in the suggestion box, private correspondence, bars, advice to friends and relatives, complaints to the city council and, of course, personal essays.

If you want to get something off your chest and feel that you are skilled enough for the job, there's no reason why you shouldn't give it a try in essay form. In fact, some newspapers and magazines have recently introduced opinion sections in which citizens can let off steam on a variety of issues. Most of these published views come from established writers, scholars, statesmen, etc., but every now and then a plain, ordinary citizen gets to speak his or her piece. Their topics have included women's lib, the inequities of Social Security, the high cost of college, gun control, the decline of railroads, East-West relations and hitchhiking. They are a welcome departure from the heavy, somewhat formal sentiments often put forth by academics and other specialists.

But there are rules for the opinion essay. One is that you present your thesis with more light than heat. However strong your opinions are, they must emerge clearly and coolly. Second, your views will be more convincing if they are buttressed by fact and authority. If you show an understanding of the issue, offer your view compellingly, and have the data to back you up, you'll make a sound case. Say you're expressing an opinion favoring some kind of national health insurance. If you can bring in the names of a couple of prominent doctors who agree with you, your opinion carries more weight. The same would be true of an anti-health insurance stand.

Historical evidence also helps. One reason that the late Walter Lippmann was a great columnist was that he had a fine sense of history and was able to wrap his judgments in historical context. If you don't know what's happened before, it's difficult to gain a clear perspective for the present and future. This could be as true of a company problem as of world affairs. If the boss wants an opinion on whether to develop new markets abroad, it would be prudent to learn if previous attempts in this direction were made by your firm or others and, if so, what the result was.

The following is an excerpt from a syndicated column by Joseph Kraft. Note how he marshalls opinion, fact and an understanding of history.

PARIS—Valéry Giscard d'Estaing has gone out on a limb with his proposal for a trilateral international conference on energy. A little sawing by President Ford at the summit meeting in Martinique this weekend could cause the French president a painful tumble.

But it is past time to introduce some generosity into Franco-American relations. The right American move is to accept the proposal in principle and to seek in exchange a more cooperative French position on energy problems in general and on the Arab-Israeli conflict in particular.

Giscard d'Estaing's proposal is basically that there be an early meeting among oil producers, the developed countries that consume oil, and the under-developed oil-consuming nations. Among other things, the conference would try to stabilize, and maybe lower, the price of oil; arrange for recycling, or rein-vestment, of the massive sums now being accumulated by the oil producers, and try to link oil prices to the prices of other commodities.

The first trouble with this proposal is that there has been little preparation among the developed nations. A plan proposed by Henry A. Kissinger for joint action is just getting off the ground. But there is no agreement on the right price to seek, or how it would be related to other commodities, and still less on who would bear the risks of financing the huge flow of oil money. At least a part of the reason for the lack of progress is that France, alone among the major developed countries, has refused to join the international energy agency proposed by Kissinger.

The Argumentative Essay

Expressing an opinion is not necessarily the same as advocating a cause. In writing an argumentative essay, the author is usually advancing a position—beating the drum for a political philosophy, a social theory, an economic solution or the notion that one baseball team is better than another.

In this kind of essay, you need not make any pretense of being open-minded. You are not only taking a side but attempting to line up others on the same side. It's a missionary role.

However, the writer who uses bombast to plug his case seldom wins many converts. Effective arguments are backed by solid facts. Remember, no one is obligated to take your word for anything. You must look for data that will make your argument sound and plausible, if not desirable. If you're blowing the horn for free tuition at state universities, you should marshall facts to show that the state's economy would not suffer unduly if such a plan were initiated. This is undoubtedly a counterargument opponents would use.

One ploy in argumentative writing is to first examine the opposite viewpoint, discuss whatever merits it has, and then proceed to demolish it as a whole. Next, advance your position, pointing out why it's superior to the other. Again, hit them with fact after fact. If you've done your research, you should be able to make a forceful, intelligent presentation.

Newspaper editorials offer excellent examples of argumentative writing. In most instances, they are written clearly and concisely and are ably documented. This one from the *Los Angeles Times* gives the idea:

It seems highly improper for three members of the U.S. Civil Service Commission, the very officials who administer the federal government's system of hiring based on merit, to recommend job applicants because of personal or political considerations.

But that is what has happened at least 35 times in the last six years, according to letters and memoranda made available through discovery proceedings in a suit against the commission. Although it is not known what effect the recommendation had, or even whether the applicants were hired, the referral practice reeks of influence peddling, and clearly is at odds with the very important principle of hiring on the basis of merit.

Anthony L. Mondello, the commission's general counsel, says there is no rule that prohibits the commissioners from making such recommendations. He concedes, however, that the commissioners are in especially sensitive positions and are expected to set an example of fairness in overseeing government hiring.

That is the point, of course. For some reason, it seems to have eluded the commissioners. They have not had the good sense or judgment to avoid even the appearance of impropriety.

The commissioners, Mondello says, are now considering a rule that would prohibit them and others from recommending persons for federal employment. Existing law forbids patronage in civil service hiring, and the commissioners may have violated the spirit of the law.

They are now in the rather awkward position of adopting a policy directed at their own awkward conduct in office. If they are uncomfortable, they should be. Their embarrassment aside, it is now appropriate for the commissioners to put an official end to the referral practice and, in so doing, to set an example of fairness in overseeing government hiring.

When using statistics to bolster your argument, don't run amuck. Bring out only those which are absolutely necessary to the case. An avalanche of numbers or other data may defeat your purpose by boring the reader to the point of hostility. It's also wise to go easy on sarcasm and invective. If you bear down too heavily, the reader may put the opposition in an underdog role. This lessens the effect of your argument, no matter how meritorious it is.

The Critical Essay

Most of us have a critical bone. If we read a book, hear a concert or see a movie, TV show, legitimate stage drama or musical comedy, we make judgments, even though we may not express them in writing. Most often, the judgment takes the form of saying or thinking "I didn't like it," "It was lousy," "Wow, what a play!" or "It's the same old stuff." There are even more general impressions such as "It was okay" or "It wasn't bad."

In writing a critical essay, you've got to narrow your judgment down. It's not enough to say whether you like or dislike a book or performance. The reader wants to know *why*? What factors determined your verdict? How does it compare with other plays, books or concerts in the same category? What was the author trying to say and how well did he or she say it? Are there special circumstances which influence your criticism? Say, for example, you have read a book on an important social topic such as alcoholism, crime, drug abuse or nursing homes. The author is not much of a stylist but has important ideas to contribute. Therefore, the book should be evaluated primarily on content. By the same token, an allowance might be made for a writer's first novel if it shows unusual promise. If, in his fourth novel, the promise is unfulfilled, that ought to be noted, too.

Since criticism is opinion, the critical essay or review can be quite subjective. After all, it's how you see a book, painting, dance, play, etc. The reader is free to disagree with you but he can't, in good conscience, fault you if your review is honest, intelligent and well considered. It also helps if you have some qualifications for passing judgment. If one has read only three books in his lifetime, his appraisal of a novel is of questionable value. If an individual has no background in music, is he competent to critique a symphony performance? Keep in mind that a number of readers may themselves have musical experience or training. They can easily spot someone who doesn't know what he's talking about.

Expertise by itself does not ensure readable criticism, however. I have read book review manuscripts by top authorities on the subject matter. Some of these efforts were hopeless in terms of style, organization and simple understanding. They were cluttered with jargon, saturated with ninety-word sentences and even contained numerous mis-spellings. An expert on nuclear energy could not write plainly about it. Frequently, book editors of newspapers and magazines would rather assign a review on a technical subject to a generalist than a specialist when they know the former will turn out readable prose.

Drama, movie and television critics for the mass media usually qualify as experts, but if you read them carefully, you will note that their sentences and paragraphs are sharp and clear. They labor on the assumption that the reader may want to see the play himself and seeks some kind of guidance before he plunks down his twenty dollars for two orchestra seats.

Whatever else you do, don't be arch or condescending in the critical essay. It's entirely possible to opinionate without sounding like a literary stuffed shirt. If it's a play or book, don't forget to summarize the plot or central idea. Some reviews rattle on and on without ever giving a single clue to what a novel or play is all about. You don't have to render a detailed account of every twist and turn in the story, but the reader should have some picture in his mind when he finishes your critique. If a novel is about a young Puerto Rican immigrant who becomes a doctor through his sister's sacrifices, your review should bring this out. If a movie concerns a compulsive gambler and his problems in getting out of debt, that idea must appear in your essay. Here is a review of a musical by Kevin Kelly of the *Boston Globe*. Note how he sails right into the nub of the production and gives his views clearly and interestingly:

> "Shenandoah" at the Colonial, is absolutely magnificent. If that sounds like the conventional type of a deadlining critic, I hope you'll forgive me but more importantly, remember what I said: absolutely magnificent. Having seen it in its summer tryout at the Goodspeed Opera House, I am in danger of repeating my initial praise. I don't want to do that because, well, in my ears, I sound tongue-tied. So you'll have to accept absolutely magnificent. Accept it and rush to the Colonial where you'll see what is likely to be the best American musical of the season.

Adapted by James Lee Barrett, Peter Udell and Philip Rose, from Mr. Barrett's 1965 movie, the musical's book is a hard-headed examination of the insanity of war, in this case the Civil War and its devastating effect on a widowed patriarch, Charlie Anderson, his six sons, his daughter and daughter-in-law. Charlie Anderson is the rockbed hero of the American spirit, a farmer with 500 acres in the Shenandoah Valley, the kind of man who made this country strong. But he is, in no way, the typical patriot. He is, in fact, a pacifist, an isolationist who would keep himself and his family out of the war. But try as he does to remain apart, to shelter what is his from the howl of madness around him, Charlie Anderson stands on the slipping soil of a national holocaust.

The script is one of the most searing antiwar statements I've encountered in the musical theater. For once, we have a traditional musical, admittedly old fashioned in its format, that tells us something about the suffering human spirit and tells it with flat-out honesty and considerable eloquence, all of which, let me add, is perfectly reflected in the score by Gary Geld and Mr. Udell. Behind the Andersons' story is a lesson about the shaping of our nation, the lesson of a maverick who knows the ultimate futility of shooting strangers which, as Charlie says, is a definition of war. Strictly speaking our country may not have been built by the Charlie Andersons, but they are clearly our conscience.

I'm aware right here, that I may be making "Shenandoah" sound heavy and grim. Let me correct or, rather explain the impression. It is full of harsh truth and hard irony, but that is only one side of the Anderson's full and loving life. We come to know them in their moments of struggle and their moments of ease. For most of the first act they're a heart-warming and entertaining clan, then, in the second act, their world comes apart. All of this is told with remarkable skill, notably in the superb pace of Mr. Rose's direction; the moss hung cutout scenery by C.

Murawski; the mood-perfect lighting by Thomas Skelton; and the virile choreography by Robert Tucker. . . .

Some critical essays must be short, yet capture the essence of, say, a book. Timothy Foote manages this feat nicely in this *Time* magazine review:

LUMBERJACK. Paintings and story by William Kurelek. Unpaged. Houghton Mifflin. $6.95. Painter Kurelek worked in Canadian lumber camps after World War II to help pay for a taste of the artist's life in Paris. Since lumbering nowadays is largely done by tree harvesters that can cut 40 cords of wood in eight hours, Kurelek has drawn and written his way into the past. After the flapdoodle and sheer flapjackery often associated with lumberjack nostalgia, Kurelek's quiet combined memoir and illustrated how-to book (notching trees, washing socks, grinding axes, dynamiting log jams) is refreshingly simple, grubby and authentic. Some of his paintings have a crabbed look, as if done by a Peter Bruegel with arthritis of the drawing hand, but they open an affecting window on the life and times of lumbermen in the Northern bush.

The General Essay

To many of us there comes a time when we want to write about a subject close to our heart. The topic may not be earthshaking or even important. Still, we want to get it off our chests, to express ourselves and perhaps to dwell on a matter that seldom receives attention. We may want to write about the changing leaves in autumn, the fact that big band music is disappearing or the sights one sees while jogging at 6:00 A.M. Many of these essays in magazines and newspapers involve memories of things past—the way it was at Coney Island or in that small town in Indiana. Nostalgia inspires many essays.

High school and college assignments often ask for an essay on a subject of the writer's choosing. Unfortunately, too many of these efforts are trite and banal. They leave

the reader with the feeling that the author had little or no
interest in the theme and was only concerned with putting
a certain number of words on paper. The same is true of
essays written for college and job applications. I suggest
these guidelines for the general essay:

1. Bring a fresh, personal insight to the topic.

2. Keep yourself in the background as much as possible unless the essay is a personal memoir.

3. Don't make it too long. When you run out of
   things to say, stop.

Exercises

1. Write a personal experience essay of one thousand words. Remember the guidelines.

2. Write a five hundred-word opinion essay on a
   subject you have researched.

3. Write a thousand-word argumentative essay on a
   subject about which you feel strongly.

4. Pick out a review of a book, drama or movie from
   a newspaper or magazine. Explain why it is a
   good or bad review.

5. List five subjects about which a general essay
   could be written. Defend your choices.

CHAPTER SEVEN

The Longer Composition

For a writer, nothing is more fearful than a blank sheet of white paper. He sits at his typewriter, stares at the paper and wonders how in the world he will ever fill it. For some authors, this may call for two or three walks around the block, a rearrangement of desk drawers, sharpening pencils—anything to keep from looking at that blank piece of paper. And doing something about it.

Although even professional writers experience this trauma, it need not be so bad. If you're stuck with a long composition, don't panic. There are ways of making the task easier. Follow these rules:

1. Narrow the topic

2. Determine the research possibilities

3. Organize the material

4. Write a first draft

5. Write a final draft

Narrow the Topic

Choosing a subject for a composition is something like walking into a department store. If you have no particular purchase in mind, you may well spend an hour or more going up and down escalators and poking around on each floor. If, on the other hand, you want an umbrella, the job is simple and brief. You head straight for the umbrella section, pick out the one you want and go on your way.

If a topic is assigned, you have part of your problem solved. If the choice is up to you, the department store analogy comes into play. Beginning writers tend to think big at first. They select cosmic subjects like winning the west, juvenile delinquency, the Mississippi River, the Crusades, American presidents, women's liberation, sports in America or the growth of the suburbs. These are fine for starters, but much too broad for reasonable handling. All should be narrowed down to manageable size. Instead of winning the west, focus on Custer's final battle with the Sioux. Juvenile delinquency can be broken down into numerous segments, including drugs, gang wars, alcohol, street crimes, rehabilitation procedures, etc. One particular neighborhood project could easily produce enough material for a four thousand-word composition. And rather than traverse the entire Mississippi, why not write about the paddle-wheel steamers and their passing?

When you have a major topic, write it at the top of a sheet of paper. Then list the possible categories of the topic. The movie industry, for example, could be sliced into a number of parts: early days of filmmaking, the star system, the epic film, great directors, musicals, message movies, westerns, the evolution of the gangster movie, famous comedians, cinematography, censorship, horror films, impact of television, etc.

Put your general topic at the top of an imaginary upside-down pyramid. The top may contain such blockbusters as war, peace, immigration or communism. But as you go down the pyramid, these issues could be reduced to the War of 1812, the arms limitation agreement, Italian immigrants and Chinese collective farms. Even the latter divisions are capable of being further splintered.

Your own interest should have a strong bearing on your selection. If you're going to commit yourself to several days or weeks of research and writing, you may as well pick something that turns you on. Let's assume you are assigned the comprehensive subject of ecology. Perhaps you're a hiker or camper. You could tackle the problem from the aspect of what campers and hikers can do to preserve the balance of nature. First, it's a subject you already know something about and, second, you will probably enjoy the research and interviewing. The same might be true of the subject colonial America. If you're interested or involved in the theater, you might explore the role of plays or dancing in colonial life.

When you restrict your term paper or theme, you're doing exactly what trained scholars do. Glance at the curriculum catalog of any university. Notice how disciplines such as English, history, political science and sociology are split into various courses on different aspects of the subject. There is, of course, a general introductory course, but then the specialization begins. Political science scatters into political theory, urban politics, political parties, the Constitution, etc. Political scientists have published numerous papers, articles and books on segments of these subcategories.

A current textbook on American history breaks down one chapter, "Making of Industrial America,"* into nine different sections:

1. The Great Transformation

2. Rationalization

3. The Railroad Age

4. Dislocations and Adjustments

5. Workingmen in an Age of Industrialization

6. The American Melting Pot

7. Cities in an Industrial Age

8. Schools in a Changing World

9. What Historians Have Said

The immigrant tide, immigrants in an industrial society, the movement to restrict immigration, Slavic immigration and immigration and the generation gap—any one of these subjects could be easily expanded into a full-blown composition. Your daily newspaper does not consist of one long story embracing all of the day's news. Rather, the items are separated by type. Foreign news is delivered into separate packages labeled Middle East, Europe, Latin America, India, etc. And these are broken down further.

---

*Robert E. Burns, *Episodes in American History* (Lexington, Mass.: Ginn and Company, 1973).

When you write the longer composition, think in terms of particles, not boulders.

Determine the Research Possibilities

When you've settled on a subject for your composition, start thinking of your information sources. No one will be interested in a top-of-the-head report. Facts and documentation are essential ingredients in the paper.

Virtually any topic can be researched in libraries, but there can be problems. Small-town or branch libraries may not have the references you need. A number of school libraries are less than adequate. Nevertheless, they are starting places. First, check the card catalog. This is an alphabetical listing of the library's collection of books filed according to authors, titles and subject matter. Some systems are more elaborate than others, but books by title and author can be found in any catalog. The letters and numbers in the left-hand corner of the card tell the shelf location of the book. If you're permitted into the stacks, it's normally an easy job to find the volume. If not, fill out a catalog slip and give it to the librarian. While you're waiting, you might use the time seeking out other reference material: magazines, pamphlets, brochures, etc.

The worst times for library research are weekends and school vacations. Everyone seems to be after the same sources, creating a crunch that may leave you out in the cold. Try a quiet Monday night, weeks before your paper is due.

The *Reader's Guide to Periodical Literature* is second to the card catalog as a lucrative source of information. The *Guide*, which runs from 1900 to the present, includes only major American magazines. It is issued semimonthly, monthly, yearly and in special volumes covering three to five years. Material can be found by author, subject and title, but be sure to check cross-references. If a subject does not appear under one heading, keep looking. Even if it does, there still may be much more to find.

Let's assume your topic is Ralph Nader, the consumer advocate. Of course, you would first turn to his name. Your potential would be far from exhausted. Other headings likely to yield material would be consumerism, automobiles, fraud, law, Congress and courts. During my research for a book on presidential press relations, I discovered references under fourteen different headings in the *Reader's Guide*. Other useful periodical guides are:

1. *Poole's Index to Periodical Literature*, 1802 to 1906. Contains references to both American and British magazines.

2. *Social Sciences and Humanities Index*, 1907 to present. (Before 1965 the title was *International Index of Periodicals*.) This is more inclusive than the *Reader's Guide*, containing a number of scholarly and technical references and also foreign publications.

3. *Annual Magazine Subject Index*, 1907 to 1949. This has more than a hundred subject headings from British and American periodicals in alphabetical order. It lists some magazines not found in the other guides.

Don't stop there. Libraries have many other periodical indexes in such areas as drama, medicine, agriculture, law, the social sciences, public affairs, engineering, religion, etc. Indexes to Black publications also are available.

The more progressive libraries have microfilming files to save space and provide researchers with an easier means of getting information. Most microfilming is of newspapers and magazines, although some books and other materials are on film. Before you run film, know at least the approximate date a newspaper or magazine article appeared. Otherwise, you could roll through three or four years of a daily newspaper before hitting your target. This takes time a writer can ill afford. The *New York Times Index* is an exact-date source for issues of that publication, which refers to itself as a newspaper of record. Presidential speeches, press conferences and all historic events are likely to receive more complete coverage in the *Times* than in any other newspaper. Other major reference sources are the *Washington Post*, the *Los Angeles Times*, the *Chicago*

Tribune, the *Christian Science Monitor* and the *St. Louis Post-Dispatch.* Access to the morgue or library of newspapers is difficult unless you know a staff member who can obtain permission for you. But that shouldn't stop you from trying.

Additional library help is contained in the special shelves or tables of new fiction and nonfiction, bulletins, brochures and other reading matter.

When consulting a reference book, be sure to check the author's bibliography. This can spare you hours of work which the writer already has done for you. His sources become your sources and those can lead to still more references.

The library is only one source of information. In our media-oriented society, the possibilities for knowledge are enormous. One of the richest lodes is in Washington, D.C., where the federal government puts out hundreds of pamphlets on everything from canning pears to home construction. The Government Printing Office provides free, or at a small charge, booklets on agriculture, social welfare, business practices, nutrition, sanitation, lumbering, gardening and scores of other matters. States, counties and some cities hand out similar publications.

Many corporations, associations, foreign embassies and consulates, private foundations and other organizations can also be considered as research resources. My daughter received free of charge a wealth of material from the Indian embassy in Washington for a high school paper she was doing on India. Business and industrial corporations have reams of data on their operations. It's yours for the asking. The information, which usually emanates from public relations departments, is self-serving but that doesn't necessarily mean that it's not useful. Just be sure to read it with a critical eye.

Organize the Material

Two kinds of organization are involved here. First, your notes and the other fruits of your research must be put into some order. When you need a fact, you want to know where it is. A convenient method is to place data on 3-by-5-inch file cards, which can be arranged alphabetically or by subject. Whole books have been written with this system and it should work for you. But it's not the only way. Pick out a procedure with which you are most comfortable. The important thing is that facts be easily available to you as you are writing. Some writers prefer to put their notes on regular size paper and keep them in folders. This is especially handy if your accumulation includes newspaper clippings and other printed matter. I know one successful author who uses shoe boxes, labeling them according to their contents. He's still trying to solve the space problem, however.

Second, you must plan the overall organization of your paper. Let's say your subject is volunteer fire departments. The paper could be developed this way:

1. An introductory paragraph describing the status of these departments today, noting particularly any conflict surrounding them.

2. Detailed case studies of one or two typical volunteer units.

3. The diminishing importance and status of volunteer departments as many rural communities have grown into crowded suburbs.

4. An assessment of volunteer fire departments by experts in the field. How do they compare with paid, professional firemen?

5. The future of volunteer fire departments as America continues to become more urbanized.

This is a general outline. A number of elements would be used to fill it out. For example, the comments of volunteers and property owners in communities with volunteer fire departments should be solicited. These would add both human and factual touches to the article. A case history or two of a volunteer force fighting a fire would add still another dimension. The important thing is that you develop a structure for the composition before you begin writing.

The opening paragraphs should command immediate attention. A dull or flat beginning will lose readers. And even if an instructor must wade through it all, a ho-hum lead may predispose him against the entire piece. Your starting sentence should amuse, delight, surprise, outrage or pique the curiosity of the reader. It must make him want to go on. Here is the way James Nathan Miller began a *Reader's Digest* article on airline safety:

This is the ominous, behind-the-scenes story of two recent fatal airplane crashes. Both might have been avoided if safety officials had done their jobs. And the record indicates that there will be more such avoidable accidents so long as the Federal Aviation Administration, which is supposed to police aviation, continues to let the industry police itself.

In his narrative about the great blue shark, Phillipe Cousteau begins:

His entire form is fluid, weaving from side to side; his head moves slowly from left to right, timed to the rhythm of his motion through the water. Only the eye is fixed, focused on me, circling within the orbit of the head, in order not to lose sight for a fraction of a second of his prey or, perhaps, of his enemy.*

Don't let the fact that your subject is of a technical or scholarly nature sway you toward heavy, pretentious lead paragraphs. In fact, ponderous wordage should be avoided throughout your composition. Instead of impressing people, as is usually intended, such a style will put them to sleep.

After you've composed your beginning, a lot more work lies ahead. Write a first draft and then ask yourself these questions:

1. Does the composition follow a logical pattern? Is there a well-defined beginning, middle and end?

2. Is then main idea clearly expressed?

---

*Jacques-Yves Cousteau and Phillippe Cousteau, *The Shark* (Garden City, N.Y.: Doubleday & Co., Inc., 1970), p. 1.

3. Does the composition build as it goes along? Does each paragraph carry on the idea of the one above it?

4. Are claims and assertions supported by solid documentation?

5. Are there inconsistencies? Do you say one thing on page 2 and contradict it on page 10?

6. Are there loose ends? Is everything explained that should be explained?

7. Are the spelling, grammar and punctuation correct?

8. Is there "extra baggage" in the form of unnecessary words, sentences and paragraphs? This can break the smoothness of the work.

9. What about vocabulary? Have you repeated the same word over and over? Can some $10 words be changed to 50-cent ones?

10. Is there an adequate bibliography and are the bibliographic references in the right place?

Write a First Draft

In my years of teaching writing courses, one memory stands out: very few students write more than one draft. And it shows.

Writing is a polishing process as any professional will tell you. It was reported that the late novelist and short story artist John O'Hara wrote only one draft. But O'Hara had written for many years before he achieved that skill. For most authors, two or more drafts are absolutely essential.

Consider the first draft a run-through. If you have an outline, follow it as closely as possible. To save time, you might leave out long quotations, simply marking where they go on the page. Don't worry about neatness the first time around. If there are typos, crossouts, spelling errors, etc., don't spend much time going over them on a sentence-by-sentence basis. They will be corrected in a subsequent draft. The writer's enthusiasm is usually highest for the initial draft. He shouldn't lose his momentum. Write as rapidly as you can and *for as long a period as you can.* One of the problems of writing is remaining seated long enough to finish what you start. Turning out a page or two one day and then adding another one three or four days later is not the best way to do it. It can lead to choppiness and disorganization. It might not be possible to finish a paper at one sitting, but come as close as you can. If you complete three or four pages one night, take the cover off the typewriter the next morning and keep going. If you stall too long, you may lose your zest for the project. One fact is certain: it won't get any easier by putting it off.

Another advantage of sustained writing is that ideas are fresh in your mind, as is the total picture of your composition. Shelve the assignment for two or three weeks, and the point becomes elusive. When you pick it up again, it doesn't seem the same. It's often a good idea to sleep on your first draft—but first it must be fashioned.

Write a Final Draft

The number of drafts you write depends on your skill, experience, mood, ambitions and other factors. As mentioned earlier, I've found students reluctant to go beyond their first draft. At least one more is essential. Your final draft should meet high standards of organization, neatness, style, grammar, punctuation, interest, documentation and meaning. In composing the last draft, take care to:

1. Rearrange the sequence if the organization is faulty.

2. Straighten out awkard sentences.

3. Substitute bright, scintillating phrases for flat ones.

4. Check words for ease of understanding. Change obscure ones to plain ones, general ones to specific ones.

5. Go over the punctuation, making sure the commas, periods, quotation marks, possessives, etc., are in the right place.

6. Examine the paper for omitted words, paragraphs or references. It's fairly common to accidentally skip a sentence or paragraph while writing.

7. Tighten loose sentences and paragraphs. Sometimes it takes three or four drafts to accomplish this.

8. Double check to be certain that sources are identified and statements authenticated.

Better results are achieved by typing the last draft yourself. It's possible to edit while you type. Professional authors who can afford the best typists on the market often write their own final drafts.

When can you say you're finished? If the paper has met the above tests, you're on pretty safe ground. The hardest person to fool is yourself. If you don't take pains with your effort, you can bet it's in for trouble when an expert goes over it. Why not eliminate the risk by being honest with yourself?

This "A" paper by a graduate student embodies the highest qualities of research, style, organization, clarity, interest and documentation. Read it carefully:

AN AMERICAN EVE

The Woman Pioneer on the Frontiers of Time

By Barbara Moore Lee

i.

Eudora Welty has achieved for the American novel the crystallization of a new venturer in a new American adventure. Four interrelated Welty novels articulate the experience of the pioneer in our last terrestial frontier: a frontier not of space, but of time. Unlike the American Adam so admirably defined by R. W. B. Lewis, this migrant in time cannot view American life and history as just beginning. Unlike the American Adam, this is an American Eve. And she is Eve after the fall, who, expelled from the garden, must cope with the shock of one of the world's prime examples of cultural change. Welty's Eve, like Milton's, must go forward, but she looks back. Her dilemma is which of the values and memories of the past she should jettison, and which she should try to take with her.

The novels take place in a present still heavily encumbered with the past, at that trembling moment of balance before the present is replaced by the future. They share much else in common: in use of character, social situation and story line. *The Optimist's Daughter* (1972) is a direct successor of *The Ponder Heart* (1954), and *Losing Battles* (1970) is a direct succesor of *Delta Wedding* (1946).

To speak of story lines as even existing in the Welty novels is, I am aware, an act of mild critical heresy, for over and over again the Welty opus has been described (even while being described admiringly) as consisting of perhaps one part plot to nine parts talk. It is also heretical to speak of the existence of social consciousness and commentary in her fiction, for she has been criticized both in print and in person for a failure to treat vital issues of the day, notably the relationship between whites and blacks in the South, but also, by extension, Vietnam, pollution, the H-bomb, women's lib, politics. For that matter, it is slightly heretical to discuss the Welty novel at all, for Miss Welty is consistently hailed as a master of the lyrical short story, but not of the novel. Things she does so well—capture the nuances of speech, scrutinize modes of family living and loving, and write fine short stories—may have tended to overshadow her plots, her social commentary, and her novels.

This will change, for the appearance of two major Welty novels after a fifteen-year publishing hiatus will inevitably result in at least a temporary shift of critical interest from the Welty short story to the Welty novel. With the publication of *The Optimist's Daughter*, the total by some criteria reaches six, as stories in her collection *The Golden Apples* (1949) are regarded by many critics[1]

---

[1] For example, Ruth M. Vande Kieft, *Eudora Welty* (New York: Twayne, 1962), p. 111; Alfred Appel, Jr., *A Season of Dreams: The Fiction of Eudora Welty* (Baton Rouge: Louisiana State Univ. Press, 1965), p. 205; or Frederick J. Hoffman, *The Art of Southern Fiction: A Study of Some Modern Novelists* (Carbondale: Southern Illinois Univ. Press, 1967), p. 63.

as being so closely linked as to form a novel. Also, her frontier fairy tale, *The Robber Bridegroom* (1942), is certainly a novel, although so special in mode that it stands to one side of her evolutionary line. Nevertheless, a major element that Miss Welty has mined so successfully in her four mainstream novels is also present in these works: the antipodes of past and future, and how to reconcile them in a rapidly changing society.

i i.

A lengthy digression in *The Robber Bridegroom* sets up the theme of coping with changes brought by time. Primeval forests are becoming cultivated fields, muses a Welty American Adam, Clement Musgrove, and his wife, Salome, concurs: "The settlement has come and the reckoning is here." (*Bridegroom*, p. 144).[2] The reckoning is more fully explored in the next novel, *Delta Wedding*, and the Welty patterns begin to emerge. A brief review of the novels that will be given here is, I warn, not a well-rounded summary, but is deliberately limited to a demonstration of the two chief devices Miss Welty uses to investigate man's relation to time. These devices are (a) the outsider who tries to uproot someone from a clan situation and (b) the outsider who disrupts a family which is in decline.

In *Delta Wedding*, a family gathers for one of life's big moments, a wedding. The daughter of an old plantation family, Dabney Fairchild, is going to marry Troy Flavin, a social and geographical outsider from the Mississippi hill country. Change thereby threatens. But in the central story line, the threat of change is already apparent: Robbie Reid, a girl locally underfoot but a social outsider, fiercely resents what seems to her the allegiance of her husband, George Fairchild, the family hero, not to her as an individual but to the group—the extended family, consisting of aunts and great-aunts, brothers and sisters, nieces and nephews, and a galaxy of great and great-great forebears, those symbols of family tradition whose physical presence

---

[2] Page references cited in parentheses throughout the text refer to standard editions of the Welty works, in this case the Doubleday, Doran and Co. edition of *The Robber Bridegroom* (New York, 1942).

is still viable in both their artifacts and in the memories of the present Fairchild generations. Robbie wants George for herself alone, in a nuclear-family cell, consisting of husband, wife, and their possible offspring. Perfection for Robbie is a small apartment, not a sprawling, tradition-ridden family home. Perfection is the city, not the rural area. In one way to read the novel, Robbie battles, in short, for movement from a rural agrarian past, in which the extended family functioned as a mutual protection system, to the isolation of the urban environment, a movement industrialization and urbanization are urging world-wide.

The closing scene of the novel strikes a note of happiness and peace, but there are heavy overtones that say change has been only temporarily averted. A partial outsider, Ellen, mother of eight Fairchilds but herself "the opposite of a Fairchild," (*Wedding*, p. 20)[3] has earlier had occasion to think, while pondering family catastrophes which have so far just missed happening, "For a little while it was a charmed life. . . . " (*Wedding*, p. 166) And in the final paragraphs an insider, a young Fairchild, stands looking at a river (one of the many time symbols used in the novel) "as if she saw some certain thing, neither marvelous nor terrible, but simply certain come by." (*Wedding*, p. 247)

I have referred to *Losing Battles* as the successor to *Delta Wedding*. It is. The same basic conflict is enacted. Gloria Short, like Robbie Reid, is an outsider married to the young man of her ardent choice, and like Robbie she wishes to draw him away from his rural-agrarian extended family into the nuclear-family cell. Her cry is "Home ties. Jack Renfro has got family piled all over him." (*Battles*, p. 163)[4] The social class of *Battles'* characters is not that of the Southern plantation owner but the hill-country cracker, and the big societal ritual is not a wedding but a family reunion, at which four generations are present. The honoree of the reunion is ninety-year-old Granny Vaughn, and her ancestors, just like past generations of Fairchilds, are also alive and present in the memories and

---

[3] *Delta Wedding* (New York: Harcourt, Brace, 1946).
[4] *Losing Battles* (New York: Random House, 1970).

legends of the family. Gloria's husband, Jack Jordan Renfro, is, like George Fairchild, the family's chosen hero, and,
like George, he is the material out of which, deservedly or
no, they spin contemporary legends. Just as the Fairchilds
simultaneously slight Robbie and yet attempt to draw her
into the family, the Vaughns simultaneously slight Gloria
as an outsider and try to draw her into family communion.
An orphan of mysterious parentage, Gloria is, they decide,
the illegitimate offspring of a deceased Vaughn and a frail,
feeble-witted, now-deceased local girl, a Sojourner, and
therefore, willy-nilly, she is one of them.

Gloria denies them and continues stubbornly to hope
to wean Jack from the family's bosom. A sojourner in time,
she urges change, just as her mentor, schoolmarm Julia
Mortimer, tried to bring change and progress to a community threatened with change and deterioration. But
whereas Gloria wants nothing to do with either her husband's family or "the dead old past" (*Battles*, p. 361) her
19-year-old husband finds them not a burden, but a source
of strength. The author provides a telling symbol to cast
light on his reasons: in front of the family home hangs a
wisteria-bonneted bell put up by the family's founder when
the country was new to toll lost travelers to sanctuary.
And Gloria's young brother-in-law muses, "Though no one
was lost any more, there could be no bell that does not say
'I will ring again.'" (*Battles*, p. 365)

The Ponder Heart, a short, romping comedy, establishes the second of the two basic patterns. There is no
battle here of outsider vs. teeming family. Rather, against
the outsider Welty lines up a sterile remnant of an old
family and a community. Edna Earle Ponder, heading for
spinsterhood despite still-sturdy hopes to the contrary,
realizes that she is going to outlive her Uncle Daniel Ponder
and become the last of the family, for everyone else has
either died or gone away. Further change has already
threatened the Ponder family, as Edna Earle relates. The
town, which is their family seat, has "gone down" (*Ponder*,
p. 13)[5] and a new highway now runs through the middle
of it. Worse, a conspicuous consumer named Bonnie Dee

---

[5] *The Ponder Heart* (New York: Harcourt, Brace, 1954).

Peacock has stirred the stagnant pond of the Ponders' prosperity. Like Robbie Reid and Gloria Short, Bonnie Dee is an outsider, the offspring of an old but fallen-away family. She marries addlebrained Uncle Daniel on a trial basis, but she pines when the marriage offers her only a lonely life in an isolated rural house.

We suspect, also, that marriage offers Bonnie Dee a conjugal bed in which Uncle Daniel does nothing more than genially fall asleep. Gloria Short Renfro, less than nine months after her marriage, has already produced a new member of the Vaughn lineage. Robbie (and a pair of gossipy dames who encounter her) wonders if she may be pregnant. Contrarily, Bonnie Dee, after six years of marriage, is childless. Her most vigorous role is that of a consumer of washing machines, velveteen dresses, and perfume samples for which she sends off magazine coupons. She dies, either frightened to death by a severe lightning storm, or, according to Edna Earle, tickled to death by Uncle Daniel. The unmentioned but valid threat that she will inherit the old Ponder home and the other Ponder assets therefore goes unrealized.

The novel presents two occasions for society's big gatherings—Bonnie Dee's funeral and a farcical trial in which Uncle Daniel is up on a charge of murdering the little outsider. In the process of the trial, he is acquitted, and he gives away most of the family fortune (one of his pastimes). The book ends on a note of the last two aging Ponders' having lost their place in their community; the money Uncle Daniel has given away estranges them from the townfolk.

Estrangement from the community, whether self-induced or involuntary, is the basic tension in *The Golden Apples* in which two types of characters are juxtaposed: the sojourners and the representatives of the community. It is the static, unchanging security of the community away from which its more venturesome members wander—according to the view of the community, "terribly at large, roaming on the face of the earth . . . human beings, roaming, like lost beasts." (*Apples*, p. 85)[6] *The Golden Apples*,

---

[6] *The Golden Apples* (New York: Harcourt, Brace, 1949).

whether short story collection or novel, presents such a
complexity of story lines that I shall not attempt to treat
them here. Ruth Vande Kieft has already undertaken the
task felicitously, and her study is recommended to the
reader.[7]

The Optimist's Daughter, for reasons that will perhaps best be figured out by critics who lean toward psycho-
biographies, picks up certain of the Ponder patterns and
combines them with the polemic of the individual versus
the group which runs strongly through *Delta Wedding* and
Losing Battles. The observing consciousness is not that of
a comic, gregarious Edna Earle but a dignified, withdrawn
World War II widow, Laurel McKeiva Hand, who pursues
a business career in Chicago. Her father, Judge McKeiva,
the last, elderly male member of an old and locally prominent family (in Mount Salus, Mississippi), has married
another outsider to the community, Wanda Fay Chisom. In
basic background and personality, she is Bonnie Dee, aged
forty. Like Bonnie Dee—and Laurel—Fay is childless.

The judge dies, following surgery in a New Orleans
hospital. In a mild reversal of the Ponder death scene, the
judge has been frightened to death, believes Laurel, by Fay.
For Fay, it is the present, not the past, that deserves
homage; the Carnival—or life—is going on outside the hospital windows, and Fay's version is that she has tried to
scare the judge out of dying and into living. The big societal
ritual in this novel is Judge McKeiva's funeral. Signifi-
cantly, Fay has him buried in the "new part" of the ceme-
tery, which reverberates in sympathy with passing traffic,
being "on the very shore of the new interstate highway."
(*Daughter,* p. 92)[8]

Physical threat to the McKeiva family home and tradition is realized. Fay inherits the portrait of Judge Mc-
Keiva's Confederate-general father, his copy of *The Last
Days of Pompeii,* and the house. Worse, to Laurel, Fay
inherits among other household possessions a finely crafted
breadboard made by Laurel's dead husband, Phil, for her
dead mother. The breadboard and birds are two major

---

[7] Vande Kieft, pp. 111-149.
[8] *The Optimist's Daughter* (New York: Random House, 1972).

symbols used by Welty in this novel, and the meaning Laurel attaches to them are pertinent to the whole Welty canon.

The salient passage explaining Laurel's feeling of fear and repugnance toward birds comes in her recollections of her mother's girlhood home in West Virginia, where her grandmother kept pigeons. As a small child, visiting, Laurel refused to have anything to do with them, because:

> Laurel had kept the pigeons under eye in their pigeon house and had already seen a pair of them sticking their beaks down each other's throats, gagging each other, eating out of each other's craws, swallowing down all over again what had been swallowed before: they were taking turns. The first time, she hoped they might never do it again, but they did it again next day while the other pigeons copied them. They convinced her that they could not escape from each other and could not themselves be escaped from. So when the pigeons flew down, she tried to position herself behind her grandmother's skirt, which was long and black, but her grandmother said again, "They're just hungry, like we are." (*Daughter*, p. 140)

Hungry just like people are, birds to Laurel are a trope for a disgusting and fearfully intimate human relationship — the interaction of members of a group taking turns victimizing one another, swallowing and reswallowing the undigested stuff of the emotional life.

The breadboard is a symbol of relationships possible between the human being in the present and his predecessors in the past. Laurel's migration through time requires that she somehow reconcile the vacuum of the present with the values of the past, and she does so articulately in the final scene of the novel.

The treasured breadboard has outlived its function, but Laurel would save it from Fay if the could. They clash over it, disputing its possession. The last moments of the conflict are instructive:

> "I don't know what you're making such a big fuss over. What do you see in that thing?" asked Fay.

"The whole story, Fay. The whole solid past,"
said Laurel.
"Whose story? Whose past? Not mine," said
Fay. "The past isn't a thing to me. I belong to the
future, didn't you know that?"
And it occurred to Laurel that Fay might already
have been faithless to her father's memory. "I know
you aren't anything to the past," she said. "You
can't do anything to it now." And neither am I; and
neither can I, she thought, although it has been everything and done everything to me, everything for me.
The past is no more open to help or hurt than was
Father in his coffin. The past is like him, impervious, and can never be awakened. It is memory that
is the somnambulist. It will come back in its wounds
from across the world, like Phil, calling us by our
names and demanding its rightful tears. It will never
be impervious. The memory can be hurt, time and
again — but in that may lie its final mercy. As
long as it's vulnerable to the living moment, it lives
for us, and while it lives, and while we are able, we
can give it up its due. (*Daughter*, pp. 178-9)

Having defined and thereby captured the vital essence of the past, its living memory, Laurel lets its arti-
fact, the breadboard, go. She leaves, leaving the breadboard
behind her, along with the other physical remnants of
her family tradition and the community to which she will
never again be more than a visitor. Within a few lines
the book ends with the potentially promising future — a
swarm of anonymous little first-graders — waving goodby
to her.

Over-all, a major message of the book is that the
future *is* coming, the past *is* crumbling; the only way to
utilize the past is to internalize its lessons and let its physical form go. And, the book instructs us, the wise person
picks and chooses among the lessons of the past. Mere
tradition is not enough. For instance, Fay had enacted a
hysterical scene beside the Judge's coffin, in emulation of
her mother's best coffin-side manners. A gently ironic
voice in the book points out that Fay was following

family tradition, and asks, "We can't find fault with doing that, can we, Laurel?" (*Daughter*, p. 111)

We can, and Miss Welty clearly expects us to. The very clarity of the messages announced in the novel as to what elements of the past the migrant in time can hope to take with him as he moves into the future may, in fact, damage *The Optimist's Daughter*, which has a neatness rarely encountered in Miss Welty's fiction. A bad thing about arguments in fiction, Miss Welty has written, is, indeed, the menace of neatness. She explains, "Great fiction, we very much fear, abounds in what makes for confusion; it generates it, being on a scale which copies life, which it confronts. It is very seldom neat, is given to sprawling and escaping from bounds, is capable of contradicting itself, and is not impervious to humor. There is absolutely everything in great fiction but a clear answer." [9]

But *The Optimist's Daughter* does articulate a clear answer. Similarly, that damnable breadboard may be regarded as damaging to the novel. As a major symbol, it risks bathos. Fay and Laurel, one could say, might just as well have been spatting over who gets the cup towels and the sheets. But if a clear answer and a breadboard diminish one novel, they shed useful light on the Welty credo and her delicate explorations of the human condition in an era in which one of the few certainties is that everything is going to change.

Why a breadboard? Concomitantly, why chiefly women (with the notable exceptions of George Fairchild and Jack Renfro) as major characters? It has proved tempting to many critics and reviewers to categorize Miss Welty as a "lady writer," or, worse, because it combines two targets of contemporary bigotry, the woman and the Southerner, as a "Southern lady writer," and Miss Welty's use of Southern women as major characters has no doubt contributed to this. But for the problem which she has so consistently explored, the choice of women protagonists is fully

---

[9] "Must the Novelist Crusade?" *The Atlantic Monthly*, Oct. 1965, p. 105.

appropriate. While an artist of her stature cannot be squeezed into yet another pejorative category, in Allen Tate's term that of the "sociologists of fiction," no novel can escape the society, real or imaginary, from which its characters spring, and the Welty novels focus unerringly on the peculiar nature of women's place in culture and cultural change the world over.

Listen to another woman, anthropologist Margaret Mead, who has written extensively on the subject. Here is a condensation from two of her studies of Mead's views on the role of women:

The daily routine of cooking, care of the house, and care of the children is left to the women in most societies. In rapidly changing cultures, the old religions, the old social values, the old braveries, and the old vanities may be taken away from the man, leaving them empty-brained and idle-handed, but the woman continues to cope with the routine affairs of domesticity. It is impossible to strip her life of meaning as completely as the life of the man can be stripped. A multitude of details bind grandmother to mother and mother to daughter. In effect, through day-by-day education in the handling of domestic tasks, they tend to cook liver in the same way, use the same patent medicine on a cut finger, and in the same way fasten their babies on a cradle board or carry them on the hip or plop them in a crib to keep them out from underfoot. The domestic tradition taught by one generation to the next binds women together in a set of positive habits, and, in many ways, defines their particular culture. Rural or urban, attitudes and conditions — at least until this present point in the twentieth-century — have changed very little for the domestically inclined or entrapped woman. This can result in their having a far more traditional, or conservative, attitude than that of their husbands.[10]

---

[10] Margaret Mead explores this topic in *The Changing Culture of an Indian Tribe*, Chap. VIII, "The Degree to Which Woman Participates in the Culture" (New York: Columbia Univ. Press, 1932), pp. 133-163, and, more briefly and recently, in *Culture and Commitment: A Study of the Generation Gap* (New York: Doubleday, 1970), pp. 40-41.

In the Welty universe, these traditionalists are the Aunt Tempes and Great-Aunt Shannons, the Edna Earles and Miss Beulah Renfros (Jack's mother in *Losing Battles;* Southerners long ago solved the Mrs.-Miss-Ms. confusion). Against them, on their own ground, Miss Welty pits other women who marry into the family or community tradition and act as disturbing factors, or, in another term, change agents. These are the Gloria Shorts and Robbie Reids, the Bonnie Dee Peacocks and the Wanda Fay Chisoms. Outsiders all, they represent a future that, like the weather, can be predicted and is surely coming. There is a third personage who has a foot in both the traditional and non-traditional camps. Her name is Ellen/Laurel, and both are partial outsiders, deeply conscious of the nature of change.

i i i.

Pertinent to the school of which she is considered a member is some consideration of how Miss Welty's time traveler fits into the Southern tradition in literature, and the question, so often asked (and so often answered, both yea and nay), has this tradition fallen into a decline?

One obvious connection of the Welty patterns is to Agrarianism, that concept of an Old South (based on supposedly European principles of an orderly, traditional society in harmony with its lands and resources) as opposed to a New South (scurrying toward industrialization, ever-increasing production goals, and urban blight) first defined in 1930 in *I'll Take My Stand.* The path from garden to city is obviously a major Welty concern. Further, the change motif, beginning in 1918 when industrial transformation of the South first came acreeping, has been a spur to the whole Southern renaissance, and sundry fine Southern writers have dealt seriously with the theme of change. In fact, according to one point of view, "It might be said that the grand subject of the modern Southern writers is 'The South in Transition.' "[11]

---

[11] Thomas Daniel Young, et al., eds., *The Literature of the South,* Revised Edition (Glenview, Ill.: Scott, Foresman, 1968), p. vii.

But the transition, according to many observers, has
now been completed, and with it the viability of the literary school. Here is a pair of typical opinions, first from
William Styron, then from Jonathan Yardley:

> The manners and mores of a nineteenth-century
> feudal, agrarian society collided head on with the
> necessities of an industrial civilization. The result
> of the collision . . . may have been comic or more
> often, with Faulkner at least, tragic, but it did give
> rise to a rich, viable literature. Yet now as this
> difference is erased and the contraditions smoothed
> out . . . now, in short, as the South is truly absorbed
> into the substance of the rest of the nation, I think
> that Southern writing, if it doesn't fade away al-
> together, will certainly no longer correspond to any-
> thing we recall from its illustrious past.[12]

And:

> If I am correct in guessing that *Losing Battles* is
> a work motivated in large measure by nostalgia, then
> it is nostalgia not merely for a lost South but for
> a lost Southern literature . . . *Battles* is very much in
> the tradition that began when Faulkner sat down to
> write *Sartoris*. That tradition is now four decades
> old, and dying an early death. The reason is very
> simple: the essential ingredient of the tradition is
> reverence for and understanding of the past, but
> young Southerners no longer have a past that has
> anything *unique* to teach. Eudora Welty's genera-
> tion is the last to know intimately the Southern land
> before the highways and quick-food joints took over,
> to know the Southern myth before it grew stale, to
> know the Southern family before it distintegrated.[13]

Miss Welty's response, if she cared to make one, would
be inherent in her critical theory of place, which by now
is synonymous with her name in American literature. As

12 "William Styron on Our Literature of Collision," interview by
   Phillip Rahv from *Modern Occasions*, reprinted in *Intellectual
   Digest*, March 1972, p. 83.
13 Jonathan Yardley, "The Last Good One?" rev. of *Losing Battles*,
   New Republic, 9 May 1970, p. 36.

her novels demonstrate, place, for Miss Welty, encompasses not only unique physical detail and social context, but also the persons and their pasts that have contributed to that context. "Place" thus contains not necessarily great-great-grandfather's desk made in Edinburgh and the portrait of great-great-Uncle George on his horse, but some essence of these people that is indeed unique and enduring.

In her words, "Place in fiction is the named, identified, concrete, exact and exacting, and therefore credible, gathering-spot of all that has been felt, is about to be experienced, in the novel's progress. Location pertains to feeling; feeling profoundly pertains to place; place in history partakes of feeling, as feeling about history partakes of place." [14]

Place, in the Welty credo, can also be pertinent to life, as shown in the following passage in which she was speaking about an old community:

> Indians, Mike Fink, the flatboatmen, Burr, and Blennerhasset, John James Audubon, the bandits of the Trace, planters and preachers — the horse fairs, the great fires — the battles of war, the arrivals of foreign ships, and the coming of floods: could not all these things still more with their stature enter into the mind here, and their beauty still work upon the heart? Perhaps it is the sense of place that gives us the belief that passionate things, in some essence, endure. Whatever is significant and whatever is tragic live as long as the place does, though they are unseen, and the new life will be built upon these things — regardless of commerce and the ways of rivers and roads, and other vagaries.[15]

This, then, is the essential element of her novels that has been discussed here, and this is Miss Welty's answer to the dilemma of the migrant not in a new area but a new

---

[14] *Place in Fiction* (New York: House of Books, 1957) (300 copies). Originally published in *South Atlantic Quarterly*, January 1956, p. 62.
[15] "Some Notes on River Country," *Harper's Bazaar*, February 1944, p. 156.

era, our shifting frontier of time: jettison the breadboard, but if there was something meaningful about it, remember it. Drive the new interstate highway, but let the past whisper that those six lanes of concrete were once part of the Natchez Trace, the Wilderness Road, or the Santa Fe Trail, which other pioneers, with other outlooks, traveled long before.

Though orchestrated in terms of an American Eve, the lesson is equally applicable to the new American Adam. And, in an era characterized by back-to-the-land communes and rebellion against the excesses of an industrial society — in which a few remaining clear streams or viable forests have become hotly defended treasures — the literary lesson that unique memories from a cultural past may also be worthy of being treasured does not seem moss-grown, nor the literary tradition that produced it automatically moribund.

Exercises

1. A general topic is war veterans. List five possible subdivisions that might make an acceptable subject for a composition.

2. You're writing a biography of the vice president of the United States. What reference sources are available in your community or school library?

3. Pick out a magazine article and a piece from a scholarly journal for their excellence in organization. Point out the elements that support your claim.

4. Take a theme, term paper or article that you have written within the last three years. Rewrite it with the intention of improving it.

5. The topic is the Spanish-American War. Write an outline for a 4,000-word paper.

CHAPTER EIGHT

A Matter of Mood

Time magazine carried this short item:

> You have to be born in Brooklyn to like it. And if you like it, you do not want to leave it. So the twelve children, aged eight on up, of Hugh Carey went to Albany with mixed feelings last week for their father's inauguration on New Year's Eve as New York's 51st Governor. To take his family northward, father Hugh hired a bus, and when the first roadside ALBANY sign was spotted, a cry at the back was heard: "Turn this bus around!" Arriving at the gingerbread mansion that will be their home for at least four years, the Carey kids were even more disconsolate. "Albany is an awful place, isn't it?" said one, and added, "They should change the capital to New York City. Albany has no life. Why, I don't think they even have an ice cream parlor." The Governor was more concerned with state affairs, so son Michael, 21, was delegated to be tactful: "There's been a couple of moaners and groaners, but everyone is going along."

You can readily see that this was written in a light vein in keeping with the subject matter. It was a little color added to the serious business of becoming governor of a state. An unskilled writer might have taken the incident too seriously and described it with a heavy hand.

Writing effectiveness often depends on mood. There is a right mood for different kinds of writing. Each day we take appropriate action for various facets of our lives. In winter we wear warm clothes and cool ones in summer. We laugh at some things and are sad about others. We lower our speed when driving in a rainstorm and wear dark glasses to protect our eyes from the sun.

In the same way, the writer must adjust the mood of his paper to suit the subject matter. A light, bantering tone may be called for in a piece about a Sunday picnic. Forgetting the cold chicken, the prevalence of ants, the inadvertent trespass on private property — all can be described with tongue-in-cheek exasperation. On the other hand, a paper about the pros and cons of fluoridating water does not readily lend itself to humorous or frivolous handling.

In establishing mood, I would suggest that you consider these elements:

1. The appropriate tone or mood for a paper.

2. Sustaining the mood throughout the piece.

3. The writer's point of view.

4. When to be informal.

5. When to use parody, irony and humor.

Appropriate Tone or Mood

This is a matter of common sense. It also helps if you've read a great deal by authors with different styles. Charles Dickens often wrote about tragic incidents but he also graced his pages with delightful touches of wit and irony. Arthur Schlesinger writes important and highly acclaimed books on American history and politics. Yet, he manages to weave in a great deal of human interest, color and anecdote that enlivens his thesis. Skilled authors of scientific and medical articles for a general audience can make complex and arcane developments understandable and palatable. Contrast their efforts with the formal and jargon-ridden papers in medical and scientific journals.

Perhaps a sound bit of advice is not to try anything that doesn't work well. An attempt to milk laughs from an account of mass unemployment would seem to be ill-conceived. There's not too much that's funny about being out of work. Still, it might be possible to wring a few chuckles from the experience of someone who stumbles into the wrong job and is fired after making a shambles of office procedure.

Your frame of reference for proper mood and style is usually determined by the format (thesis and dissertation readers are not generally receptive to any informality), publication and the subject. If you are writing for a particular magazine, study its content carefully. At the same time, think in terms of readability, no matter how solemn or scholarly the publication. This should hold for term papers and reports as well. It's possible to get the reader's attention without resorting to circus tactics. Just be interesting, a technique we'll take up in detail in a later chapter. For the moment, let's examine an article in *Today's Health* about mononucleosis, hardly a blithe topic. Yet the author, Dr. Michael Halberstam, manages to present it in a way that emphasizes its seriousness without anesthetizing the reader. Here is part of the article:

"Doctor, I feel like I'm dying."

The voice on the other end of my phone was Mary Pierce, the 20-year old daughter of one of my regular patients. Since I had seen Mary only once before — at a pre-college physical, when she had proved to be in excellent health — and since it is rare for women this age to suddenly expire, I didn't immediately start thinking of ambulance service numbers. On the other hand, from what I knew of Mary Pierce, she was hardly the type of woman to exaggerate symptoms.

"What exactly is wrong, Mary?" I asked, giving her as wide a latitude as possible to pinpoint her symptoms.

"Everything," she replied.

"Could you be a bit more specific?" I wanted to know.

"My head hurts, my joints hurt, I'm hot all over, my stomach aches, I can't swallow, I'm so weak that I can barely move." That more or less covered everything. . . .

Fifteen minutes later, Mary was in my office. She was, indeed, quite sick — weak, dizzy, with a temperature of 102. She had swollen, somewhat tender lymph glands all over her body, but the glands, or nodes, under her jaw and at the back of her neck were especially large. Her tonsils had a thick, whitish coating. Her skin was covered with a fine, red rash. I had already suspected the diagnosis, but Mary's history helped confirm it. . . .

"Mary, I'm 99 percent sure you've got infectious mononucleosis. I won't be sure until I get the results of the other tests back, but in the meantime, I want you to go home, stay in bed, drink plenty of fluids, take some pain medicine if you need it, and stop taking the medicine you got at school."

Mary looked anguished. "But doctor, I can't have mono. I've got a term paper to finish next month, and I'm supposed to be married in June, and I can't be sick that long."

Mary could relax. Although mono is one of the nastiest diseases around, it never causes permanent damage and almost never produces prolonged convalescence. Contrary to current folklore, most patients who have mono are back in perfect health within two or three weeks of the peak of the disease. Still, I could sympathize with Mary's concern, for although mono is not a serious disease, it is an unpleasant one, and one for which there is neither prevention nor treatment. . . .

A report on this illness would doubtless be slanted differently for a professional medical journal, but what's wrong with this way? It's informal without being flippant and it lays out the facts in a clear, readable manner.

Speaking of facts, there also is a proper mood or tone for the purely expository report. Many business or school assignments are best offered in a neutral, objective tone. There is no need for clever writing, neatly turned phrases or breezy informality. In fact, it might be harmful if you were to attempt to enliven your paper with humor, anecdote or intriguing detail which would divert attention from the central point. An example is found in this preface to an American Automobile Association guide book:

This Tour Book has been prepared primarily to make your trip more pleasant and enjoyable by providing you with accurate, detailed information about the area through which you will travel. Annual revision of all material in the Tour Books keeps you up-to-date on places of interest and accommodations. No attraction, hotel, motel, resort or restaurant pays for a listing. Attractions considered to be worthwhile and all approved establishments are listed without charge.

The *What to See* section of the Tour Books describes thousands of scenic, historic, recreational and other attractions which can add immensely to the scope of your trip. Profiles of each state and province are featured to augment your understanding and appreciation of the region you are exploring. The *Where to Stay — Where to Dine* section contains complete, authentic information on over 15,000 establishments, all recently inspected and approved by AAA Field Representatives.

Comprehensive introductory pages give a detailed explanation of the listings, tell you how accommodations are selected and explain how AAA's rate guarantee applies to hotels, motels and resorts. . . .

It's not fancy, but it tells how to use the guide book in plain terms, which it's supposed to do. In the same way, a report on the efficiency of a new machine in the plant need not be embellished with frothy prose to snare the manager's attention. He most likely prefers to seek his amusement elsewhere — not in a document upon which he depends for decision making.

One of the best illustrations of unadorned writing appears in the so-called utility or "how-to" magazines. A *Popular Mechanics* article on making a stereo cabinet will explain the steps in tight, no-nonsense paragraphs. The idea is to transmit information in the clearest, most understandable way.

Sustaining the Mood

Persistency and consistency are the marks of the accomplished writer. You must be persistent to achieve goals — finishing what you started. Consistency is equally indicative of the skilled wordsmith. The mood, tone or style must be sustained throughout anything you write. You shouldn't lead off in a gay mood that suddenly turns somber in the middle, only to switch back to lightness near the end.

We've already established that the subject usually determines the mood or tone. So, once you start with a certain mood — be it serious, ironic, mocking, funny — you must finish with it. Professional writers don't jump around with mood. They also are consistent in other ways. If Forest Avenue is used in one spot, it shouldn't become Forest Ave. on the next page. If Mr. is used with the name of one man, it should be used with the names of other people who appear in a narrative or description.

But let's get back to overall tone. Take care that you maintain the same pitch. Decide what the mood will be and then stick to it. You may think that tossing a joke into an otherwise sober analysis of ambulance service in your community will perk up your report, but don't count on it. It's more apt to throw your whole effort out of whack. There are occasions when "gallows humor" fits into a grim situation, however. Just as a joke may ease a tense situation, so will a spoonful of humor take the edge off a heavy piece of writing. In the book *A Bridge Too Far*, a serious study of the World War II battle of Arnhem, the author, Cornelius Ryan, found room for lighter moments, such as this one which occurs right after Allied troops have made a parachute landing in the battle zone:

> The first person Sgt. Norman Swift saw when he landed was Sgt. Maj. Les Ellis, who was passing by holding a dead partridge. The amazed Swift asked where the bird had come from. "I landed on it," Ellis said. "It'll be a bit of all right later on, in case we're hungry."

Reader's Digest articles often take on a chatty, homespun style. Notice how the subject of homework is approached in one article:

At the school our boys attend, the honor roll is divided into Outstanding Scholarship and Honorable Mention. We were visiting some friends one evening not long ago, and I happened to remark that Roy had made Honorable Mention. "Yeah," Al said. "The same thing happened to Curtis a few months back. There was no television for him for some time afterward, I can tell you."

The style is maintained throughout the article, which deals with the question of parents helping their children with homework. The piece could have been delivered in another style and mood — perhaps a straight, academic analysis of the value or harm resulting from homework assistance. In that case, illustration or anecdote could be employed, but rampant informality would be out of place. Professional writers do not make stark deviations in style. So, remember two steps: (1) set the mood and style and (2) follow it throughout your paper.

The Writer's Point of View

Personal journalism has come into fashion in recent years. This is where the writer brings a personal viewpoint — and even bias — into an article. Actually, there always has been room for one who seeks to impose his own stamp on a report, essay or article. Sometimes it is highly appropriate to do so. An analysis of marital problems, driving habits, drag racing, higher education or the used car business might well lend itself to a subjective treatment.

One problem with this form is that the writer may become *too* personal. The paper or report becomes an ego trip, shedding little or no light on the subject. The viewpoint style is most effective when the author is intrusive to the point of providing human interest and empathy but does not go beyond that. The idea is to report what is observed and then put it in a kind of personal perspective. An example was an article for *Ms.* magazine by a feminist writer assigned to cover the football Superbowl. She shared with the reader her rather strong views on woman's liberation while offering a fascinating insight into the hoopla surrounding the game.

The writer's point of view also finds its way into writings about politics, social change and lifestyle. Newspaper and magazine "Op-Ed" pages are crammed with articles on such topics as where people go to escape from their problems, rehabilitation of criminals, nostalgic looks at old neighborhoods and the effects of divorce. Most of these have a clearly visible viewpoint. In fact, they would probably not have been accepted for publication if they hadn't.

If you have trouble trying to decide whether or not to bring your own view or opinion into a paper, report or article, ask yourself these questions:

1. Is my viewpoint important to the piece?

2. Does the topic lend itself to personal writing?

3. Can I offer my own views and still get my idea across?

4. Is there a request for my views?

5. Will it read better if I keep my outlook to myself?

When to Be Informal

It would be easiest to say here that serious subjects call for serious treatment and lightweight topics can be dealt with informally. This is too pat a formula. There are, of course, times when levity or informality would be out of place. You would not, for example, write whimsically or gaily about starvation. Nor would you wax lyrical over deaths in highway accidents.

But a number of so-called serious issues provide a fertile field for informal handling — and could even benefit from it. There's too much stolid, solemn writing without your adding to it. Such style often translates into dullness, a malady writers should avoid. Also, you can frequently achieve greater understanding by an informal presentation, particularly if jargon is reduced or eliminated. A number of excellent writers in the areas of public affairs, politics, education, etc., develop their ideas in simple, informal language. Heavyweight political pundits such as James Reston, Mary McGrory, Marquis Childs, Joseph Kraft and Tom Wicker attract thousands of newspaper readers because of their ability to dwell on significant events in sharp, clean and generally informal prose. Here's a sample from a column by Ms. McGrory of the *Washington Star News Syndicate:*

> Congress seems on the point of turning down President Ford's "Just-one-more-time" pleas for extra funds for Vietnam. In these hard times, it is an easy, unemotional argument — "don't throw good money after bad."
>
> What it will not do any time soon, however, is deal with that other unfinished business of the war at home — the fate of those who fled, went underground or deserted. Those, in short, who with their lives endorsed Majority Leader Mike Mansfield's recently reiterated view of the war as a "tragic mistake."
>
> Ford's last minute extension of his thin-gruel "clemency" program has set off another round in the war between its principal advocate, Charles Goodell, chairman of the Clemency Board, and his critics in the antiwar movement, proponents of unconditional amnesty.
>
> Goodell is fighting an all-fronts media campaign to popularize the faltering program. His critics, led by the American Civil Liberties Union and the National Council of Churches, tell him that it is worse than nothing at all, and accuse him of trying to beef up the numbers to make the program a public relations success.

Writing informally means using the language of the people, avoiding stiffness and jaw-breaking sentences. It means writing with a certain grace and fluidity. It involves choosing words carefully to beguile the reader while informing him. Don't be afraid to lapse into idiom and slang, to use different techniques such as the diary or the second person form, and to ladle in a little humor when it suits your purpose. Forget the bulky, wooden prose that clogged many of your school textbooks. Avoid the stilted sentences of public declarations, lawyers' documents and many business letters. If you have a firm grasp of English fundamentals, let your imagination have some play. Experiment with words and sentences until they are easy to read, yet off the beaten path. Above all, make your writing *move;* give it bounce and flair. Writing about a hotel may seem like a thankless task, but observe how Paul J. Schaefer opens his piece on a famous hostelry:

> The fact that the Hotel Algonquin, one of old New York's most distinguished hotels, still offers the same hospitality that made it famous in the 20's and 30's is a small miracle. It is much as if the Baths of Caracalla were still a popular stop for jaded Romans or flotillas of showboats still plied the Mississippi entertaining the local populace. If Ethel Barrymore or Tallulah Bankhead could walk in today, as they often did in that light-hearted era, they would be completely at home, taking only a few minutes to orient themselves. For while necessary refurbishing has been done, the style and the spirit are the same.

In the hands of another writer, this could have ended up as a dry, pompous history of a hotel. If you want models for lively, informal writing, read the articles in popular magazines such as *Parade, Redbook, McCall's, Time, Sports Illustrated, Esquire,* etc. After all, if the *Wall Street Journal* can make finance interesting — and it does every day — you can inject life into your writing.

When to Use Parody, Irony and Humor

To parody is to imitate another's style, but in an exaggerated way that is designed to ridicule or spoof it. Parody is not a device that everyone can handle. It requires a delicate touch and just the right amount of stretching the original. Carried too far, parody can become an absurdity without meaning. In the hands of a skillful writer, parody can be an effective contrivance for deflating the high and mighty or for just having a little fun. Among the targets of parody have been *Time, The New York Times*, various radio and TV announcers, "Little Red Riding Hood," the *New Yorker* magazine, Gilbert and Sullivan and "Little Orphan Annie."

The main rule of successful parody is to thoroughly understand the style of the original. You can't do a take-off on the Congressional Record unless you have studied that publication closely and are familiar with its style. You might also ask yourself if your intended mark is worthy of caricature or lends itself to it. Only that which has a distinctive, widely recognized character should be considered for parody. The following spoof of a Gothic novel by the *Harvard Lampoon* is an example:

I realized I was in danger at Wolfrunt Hall the day I was pushed over the cliff.

It had become my habit to take a solitary walk while Grace was having her religious instruction with the rector of Wolfrunt-Parva, and Clarissa was having her nap. Although Wolf Heath was possibly the most dismal spot I had ever seen, it was a welcome respite from the overpowering society of the Wolfrunts, and its deathly desolation stretching unbroken to the sullen horizon encouraged the sober reflection necessary to my new and strange position in life. I had no idea what had occupied this blighted space before the war; now, of course, it bore few and stunted growths, cowering patches of a peculiarly repulsive brownish-green. It was vile.

Wolfrunt-Parva and Wolfrunt Hall itself were the only outposts of humanity, so to speak, on this blasted heath: The one was unattractively filled with the usual village louts and cretins that one finds this far from anything recognizable as civilization; the other was full of Wolfrunts, which says quite enough as far as I and the rest of the county were concerned. When I first arrived, the villagers hinted darkly of some nameless evil hovering over the Hall like a pregnant thundercloud, a mysterious curse connected with the Wolfrunt name.

Get the idea?

Webster's New World Dictionary defines irony as "a combination of circumstances or a result that is the opposite of what is or might be expected or considered appropriate (an *irony* that the firehouse burned)."

Much in life is ironic and the urge to write about it is often irresistible. Like parody, irony requires a high degree of skill. Only when you've achieved proficiency in style should you attempt it. First things first. Concentrate on writing straight, clear sentences and then branch out to the more subtle variations.

Still, almost anything is worth attempting once. If your subject has possibilities for irony, exploit them, if only to see if you can carry it off. An essay on the fuel consumption of big cars might be a suitable topic. There's also irony in the fact that certain diets may be beneficial in one way, yet harmful in another — high-protein foods, for instance. It may be ironic that the United Nations, an institution developed to promote peace and understanding, is often the scene of bitter rifts between member nations. The trick is to emphasize the irony without pounding the reader over the head with it. Let the circumstances speak for themselves. It's not necessary to say that "It was ironic that the Morris family moved to the Sahara the week after Mrs. Morris bought a fur coat." The reader will catch the irony without a complete set of directions.

The same advice applies to humor. Being funny in print is an art and one that is frequently abused. Ask yourself first if the subject lends itself to humor. Second, ask yourself if you can manage it. A number of so-called amusing pieces are in bad taste and taste is important in good writing. In addition, efforts at jollity are oftentimes strained to the point of embarrassment. Humor is created by individuals, the event or, again, circumstances. You can't force people to believe that something is funny merely by telling them that it is. Wit or whimsy must be meted out delicately, not in a slapstick manner. Slapstick worked fine in vaudeville, but you're not putting on a theater act. The finest humorists — Mark Twain,

Charles Dickens, James Thurber, Ring Lardner — were successful because of their ability to underplay characters and situations. They tickled the funnybone with a feather, not a club.

Whatever you do, don't introduce humor where it doesn't belong. What may be appropriate in a gossip column, alumni news letter or party invitation will usually not do at all for a straight business report. This doesn't mean that some term papers, essays, and theses would not benefit from a pinch of drollery — if it can be neatly slipped in. Just be sure that it fits smoothly into the particular paragraph or section you have in mind for it.

But don't worry if humor is not your strong point. Many professional writers have trouble with it and are wise enough to leave the jokes to others more adept in this area. Having a sense of humor helps, but it's not a guarantee that you can make a sentence come out funny on paper. TV comedians may seem like merry types on the home screen, but most of them would be lost without their writers.

Let me repeat: humor is best achieved when it's not forced on the reader. One of today's top humorists, Goodman Ace, is a master at this technique. This excerpt from one of his *Saturday Review* columns is an example:

> You must have read in the newspapers that the Penn Central Railroad, a going business that has been going through bankruptcy, is offering for sale twenty-eight parcels of prime, mid-Manhattan real estate, on which stands some of New York City's most famous hotels, banks, and office buildings. The asking price for this land, scattered over ten city blocks, is $1.2 billion. Cash. No trinkets. Trinkets, you recall, figured prominently in the original sale of the Isle of Manhattan. That was about 300 years ago when the white man was said by the Indians to have been born with a forked tongue. But not so Peter Minuit, a rich, fast-talking real estate operator who was born with a silver spoon in his mouth. And he had the cash to prove it.

"Well," said Peter Minuit, "it isn't exactly the location I had in mind, and I don't know if the Dutch colonists will back me up, but I'll give you twenty dollars for the whole island."

"Oh, no," said the Indian chief. "If white man offers twenty dollars, it must be worth forty dollars. I don't know if the tribal council will back me up, but you can have it for thirty dollars."

Exercises

1. Pick out an essay, short story or novel. Point out three passages in which the mood of the writing is appropriate to the situation.

2. Bring in a professional piece of writing in which the mood is sustained. What technique did the author use?

3. Write a six hundred-word factual essay in which you present a distinct point of view.

4. Write a two hundred-word informal announcement asking for volunteers to work on a neighborhood art project.

5. See if you can parody a typical *Time* magazine article.

6. It's pouring rain. You *must* run an errand. Your raincoat has just been chewed up by the dog. Your umbrella has a gaping hole. The car won't start. It looks as if your sewer is backing up. You have ten minutes to get downtown. Write a funny piece about this, adding whatever you like.

CHAPTER NINE

How Not to Be Boring

I recall a movie in which the butler in a huge mansion was vainly trying to get the attention of the master of the house, who was having a loud and bitter quarrel with several other family members. Finally, in utter desperation, the servant picked up a priceless vase and dropped it on the floor with a loud smash. The din in the room ceased immediately and all eyes turned to the butler.

As a writer, you can learn from this incident. Getting and *holding* attention is a major part of your job. Some boredom in reading is inevitable (official proclamations, insurance policies and legal documents are examples). Mainly, however, people read for interest, enlightenment or pleasure. The resourceful writer recognizes this fact and shapes his words accordingly. If the reader is bored, it's usually the author's fault. By stretching his imagination a bit and taking more care with style, he can avoid dull, plodding writing. Make your reader sit up and take notice — drop a vase!

There are devices to help you. Here are the main ones:

1. The strong leadoff
2. Use of narrative
3. Anecdote and illustration
4. Avoiding bromides
5. Raising questions

The Strong Leadoff

A successful book publisher once told a group of writers that he often spent his lunch hours in bookstores, noting the habits of browsers.

"I found," he explained, "that people bought books after reading the first page. If they read four or five pages, they usually put the book back on the shelf without buying it."

The publisher was telling the authors that if they wanted to see their manuscripts in print, they ought to think of grabbing the reader on the first page.

I have mentioned the importance of the opening paragraph in a previous chapter, but it cannot be overstressed. Readers are fickle creatures. They often form immediate judgments, sometimes to the writer's loss. You may have buried within your article, report or essay a treasury of knowledge which will never be discovered. The reader simply may not get that far.

Jolt the reader. Startle him. Horrify him. Amuse him. Intrigue him. Insult him. Flatter him. Challenge him. *But get his attention right off the bat!*

Here's an opener for an article about a man who arranges exchange visits between Russians and Americans:

One morning several weeks ago, Valentin A. Zorin, a major political commentator on Moscow TV and radio, climbed two flights of stairs of a decrepit building in midtown Manhattan. When he reached the office of the Citizen Exchange Corps (CEC), he asked a favor of its president, Stephen Daniel James. During his tour of the United States, Zorin said, he would like interviews with black leader Jesse Jackson, Mayor Richard Hatcher of Gary, Indiana, Ku Klux Klan Chief Robert Shelton, and Sen. George McGovern.

That lead is designed to instantly create reader interest. Why is a famous Russian TV newscaster seeking help in a shabby New York building? The reason is given in the second paragraph and that's the point. The reader was led to the next paragraph and to the ones beyond.

A newspaper business-page story begins this way:

Consumer delight with pressing little buttons and reading the lit-up numbers on pocket calculators is reflected in the fact that one out of ten Americans now owns one.

An essay on Valentine's Day starts out:

These days we consumers constantly hear nothing but badmouthing about trade, service and professional workers. It's always the same. "Nobody gives a damn and everyone's mainly out to get our buck!"

A travel article on Munich and the 1972 Olympics led off:

Mad King Ludwig II probably would have approved of the 20th annual Olympic Games to be held in his native city of Munich this summer. The popular Bavarian monarch (who ruled from 1864 to 1886) was, despite his eccentricities, a prodigious builder, lavish art patron and an enthusiastic supporter of games and festivals. He liked to see his people enjoy themselves.

And an opinion piece's opening shot:

The flap over a California construction company's contract to train the Saudi Arabian national guard demonstrates the remarkable ability of people to get excited over the wrong things.

These initial paragraphs all have one thing in common: they contain just enough powder to ignite reader interest. After you write your first paragraph, take a hard look at it. Does it command attention? Or will it stir only yawns in the reader? If the latter is the case, rewrite it again and again until it comes out right. It's like trying on a new pair of shoes in the store. If they don't fit, you take them off and put on another pair. You don't walk out with shoes that are too tight or too loose. At least I hope you don't.

Use of Narrative

Story telling is an ancient art that has not lost its value for today's writer. The tales you read in your early schoolbooks usually had a narrative style — stories of brave knights, fair maidens, evil demons and frogs who turned into princes.

The narrative form is proper and even preferable for *some* kinds of writing. Let's say you're part of a group attempting to raise money to preserve a historic building in your community. You might, in a narrative way, trace the history of the structure, loading your account with anecdotes and bits of old lore. You would be telling a story about the building, a story that would entertain the reader and hopefully loosen his purse strings.

Narration also can be appropriate for articles dealing with health, lifestyle, travel, current affairs, hobbies, education and many other topics. It's ideal for biographies and autobiographies and has even been used for job résumés — an appealing departure from the traditional résumé, with its vertical list of education, previous positions held, etc.

How does narrative work? The following is from a *Reader's Digest* article on hunger:

Paul Horvat couldn't believe what he saw on the television newscast. Watching at home in the Chicago suburb of Wilmette, he stared in horror as Indiana farmers — protesting low prices — burned crops, killed hogs and poured out milk. "Why should food go to waste on the farm," Horvat asked, "while people are hungry in the city?"

It was late summer of 1967, and on the next day Horvat went to Indiana, driving hundreds of miles to question dozens of farmers. What they said disturbed him: "We can't sell our crops for what it costs to raise and pick them."

A 69-year-old immigrant to America, Horvat was no stranger to social protest. In Yugoslavia, he had championed farmers' rights and fought foreign invaders through two world wars. He also knew how the Indiana farmers felt. His life as a European peasant had been a constant fight against crop failure and market supply and demand. When he got home that night, and thought about what he had seen, he knew he had to give up his comfortable land-scaping business and declare a personal war on hunger.

You can see from this how a serious problem can be presented in a familiar, homey style. Just as many facts can be jammed into a narrative form as into a straight rendition.

Still, the narrative manner has its drawbacks for certain kinds of writing. If someone wants information fast and unvarnished, he will find the story-telling technique exasperating. Business executives usually prefer memos that are short and to the point. A personnel manager inquiring about your skills may want to be spared your literary efforts and prefer that you just get down to cases.

Anecdote and Illustration

One reason for the popularity of the *Reader's Digest* is the liberal sprinkling of anecdote and illustration in its articles. Hard facts become more digestible and understandable when a vivid picture is drawn. In a piece about a devastating tornado that struck parts of the South, Joseph P. Blank, a veteran author, first described some of the general damage caused by the twister. Then he brought the tragedy into stark focus with this anecdote:

> In Brandenburg, Leck Craycroft, 53, had just re-turned with his mother-in-law from shopping and was putting the bags of groceries on the kitchen table when he heard a noise like a train. He grabbed his mother-in-law by the arm and pulled her toward the basement steps. When they were halfway down the steps, the house blew apart. Still upright, Craycroft was transported along the ground and through the debris like a small boy being carried along by his armpits. He realized he was no longer holding his mother-in-law's arm.

An anecdote is an incident, a slice of life that makes writing more vivid. It's particularly helpful in nonfiction writing because it provides a change of pace while adding something extra to an article, paper or report. Although true, anecdotes supply some of the interest and flavor of fiction to expository writing.

Anecdotes normally don't drop into a writer's lap. You've got to dig them out, either through research or interviews. A term paper on the Revolutionary War may contain a rich lode of anecdotes if you spend enough time in the library. While researching a book about the origins of the press in America, I discovered little-known stories about famous men that, in my opinion, enlivened what normally would be a straight historical account. I learned, for example, that George Washington bawled out the Constitutional Convention because one of its members lost a copy of the Convention proposals; Washington feared it would fall into the hands of a newspaper. Research also uncovered a tale about President Grover Cleveland's rage when reporters followed him and his bride to their honeymoon cottage.

If interviewing is a part of your research, probe your source for anecdotal material. If he is now famous, did he have struggles in his early years? If so, could he detail some? An athlete may tell you the toughest decision he had to make or a policeman might reveal "inside" aspects of a case — the stuff that doesn't get into the newspaper or on the police blotter. Such stories are what gives life to writing. This was brought out in a *Newsweek* profile on moviemaker Mel Brooks, which contained this anecdote:

> When Caesar moved to "Your Show of Shows," Brooks found himself the first of many jesters to the crown prince, all competing violently for Caesar's recognition. "Mel always came up with the most outrageous stuff," remembers Carl Reiner. "Late one day he started fooling with the word 'carrot.' Someone groaned, 'Not another one of those dumb eyesight jokes.' Mel was up against the wall but he was going to deliver the best carrot joke of all time. Finally, he blurted out, 'He ate so many carrots he couldn't go to sleep because he could see through his eyelids.' The joke was used on the show."

Illustrations or examples also are valuable writing aids. If you can illustrate your paper on migrant labor with a typical day in the life of a migrant family, you will have enormously increased the reader's comprehension of the issue. A report on a company morale problem would be greatly enhanced by a few illustrations of dissatisfied workers and the sources of their dissatisfaction. A description of a new high school scheduling system would need examples of how it would work in practice.

Avoiding Bromides

Old clothes are comfortable but at some point they have to be thrown out. It's the same with bromides or clichés, those ancient expressions you hear and read so often. The language is crammed with speakers who hit the nail on the head, batters who hit round-trippers, doctors who are sent on errands of mercy, students who burn the candle at both ends and criminals who are caught by the long arm of the law. These phrases and many others have served well for hundreds of years. They deserve a rest. The writer who relies on hackneyed statements runs the risk of dulling his readers. Try harder for a fresh, original phrase. If you have an adequate vocabulary, it isn't an impossible task. Find substitutes for old-timers like the following:

the weaker sex	cheering throngs
coin of the realm	bad apple (he was a)
a penny saved is a penny earned	rosy dawn
	errant fool
true to form	crack shot
ill-fated ship	man of the people
child prodigy	stiff upper lip
light at the end of the tunnel	grain of salt
	beautiful blonde
riot of color	armchair strategist

Clichés can be cast aside in favor of a plain, accepted terms. "Coin of the realm," for instance, simply means local currency. The former is a bygone relic, anyway. Feminists probably bridle at the term "weaker sex," so why not just say "women."

Few, if any, writers can entirely eliminate the bromide. Rather than sit all day in front of your typewriter brooding over a replacement for an antique phrase, go ahead and write the first thing that comes into your head. Perhaps on the next page, you'll be inspired to come up with a fresh term for another bromide.

Two means of sidestepping bromides are building your vocabulary and doing a lot of reading. Writers must be readers. You acquire standards for style and expression by reading other writers, both good and bad. You have to know what are the hackneyed terms before you start avoiding them. We pick up many of them in conversation, but there may be usages which you mistakenly think are new because *you* encountered them for the first time. In today's popular culture, new terminology quickly becomes old hat. What was "in" yesterday may be out tomorrow.

Raising Questions

Have you ever felt challenged by something you read? Did it cause you to reexamine your own beliefs and values? If so, the writer was probably quite effective — even if he didn't change your mind.

I believe most of us enjoy an intellectual challenge. We may not agree with the idea advanced, but at least it prompted us to think. You can use this technique yourself to make your writing more interesting. You don't always have to settle for the conventional wisdom. If, for example, you're doing a report on the energy crisis, you will naturally research the experts on the matter. However, make sure that you toss *your* two cents' worth in. Make your own contribution. Offer your own ideas, raise questions, and even take on the experts if their judgment seems faulty to you. Civilization was built on ideas!

This approach can be applied to different kinds of writing: essays, articles, reports and term papers. After staggering through sixty term papers in which the authors merely disgorge their reference-book findings, an instructor will most likely be delighted with one that pops up with some original thoughts. He may reject the thesis or argument while giving the student an "A" for his intellectual breakthrough.

Whether your idea shakes up the establishment or merely draws startled gasps, the effort is worth it. When you're writing to be read, get the reader's attention. The following excerpt taken from a piece in the *Los Angeles Times* meets the criterion. It was written by Gordon Davidson, artistic director of the Center Theater Group at the Mark Taper Forum.

It seems ridiculous to reargue the case for the arts. It feels like a trumped-up college debate: Are the arts Necessary for Man's Survival? Yes, of course they are — and anyone who argues otherwise deals merely in conceit. And yet, like the bald eagle and the leopard, the arts as we know them — an effective and transcendent expression produced by exceptionally gifted, perceptive, trained and disciplined people — are being wiped out.

I do not believe anyone wants this — least of all any of the participants in the discussion on this page. Nor do I believe that any of the participants here would disagree that the reason the arts are threatened is that their traditional means of support — the patronage of wealthy individuals and organizations — is no longer adequate to the task. That some form of government support is necessary to supplement the arts' traditional patrons seems obvious, and on this, too, I believe we can agree.

Whether you agree or not, Mr. Davidson has given you something to chew over, to perhaps discuss with others, to make you think. He has raised questions.

Exercises

1. Write a strong beginning paragraph for a proposed essay on the invention of the wheel.

2. Write a five hundred-word narrative account of an election day in your community or the opening day of school.

3. Pick out ten anecdotes in *Time* or *Newsweek* articles which enhance the articles. Tell why you think so.

4. In writing a report on industry's habit of moving executives around the country, what types of examples or illustrations could you use?

5. Here are five bromides. Substitute other expressions for them.

   a. Keep your nose to the grindstone.

   b. He spends money as if it's going out of style.

   c. Still waters run deep.

   d. The early bird catches the worm.

   e. He's a chip off the old block.

6. Write a challenging first paragraph for an article on the question of establishing full diplomatic relations with Communist China.

CHAPTER TEN

Writing the Business Letter

This chapter is not just about business people writing business letters. Most of us, whatever our occupations, have occasion to write business letters. We write them to the telephone company, banks, lawyers, department stores, doctors, colleges, federal, state and local agencies and numerous other places. The kind of letter you write may be important in unsnarling a problem with your credit card account or in getting a job.

For years, business correspondence was the drabest of communications. It was cursed with elaborate language, peculiar mannerisms and sometimes total obscurity. A sample of the style:

Dear Mr. Twill:

This letter is to inform you that we are in receipt of your correspondence of February 18 and have instructed our billing department to herewith examine your account with a view toward resolving the apparent discrepancy between your original order and the shipping instructions issued by our bedding department.

This kind of obfuscation still exists in much business communication, despite the efforts of some executives to weed it out. By the same token, many nonbusiness people write windy, unclear and overly formal letters every day. An individual who can write a fairly informative and even interesting social note is likely to create a monstrosity when called upon to turn out a business letter. He feels he must put on an act, inflate his usual style and become quite pompous. It's something like dressing for a special affair.

All this, of course, is nonsense. Business correspondence should be clear and straightforward. It is through business letters that profits are made or lost, applicants hired or not, orders shipped or delayed, legal information understood or misunderstood and goodwill gained or destroyed. Who wouldn't want to take great care when these matters are at stake?

The principal elements in the business letter are as follows:

1. Getting attention

2. Clarity and conciseness

3. Empathy

4. Persuasion

Getting Attention

There is a big difference between a personal and a business letter. In the first, the writer need not follow any prescribed form or style. He is free to be informal, roam freely over different subjects, display emotion and be as creative as his talents allow. The business letter is more restrictive. It has a specific objective; there are rules to follow and personal feelings are usually left out. The sender wants information, has a complaint, needs advice, is seeking employment or is trying to convince someone to buy a product. And since the recipient hasn't all day to muse over correspondence, it should generally be short.

It's important then that the first sentence draw immediate attention. It should have something definite to say. Here are some examples that might follow "Dear Mr. Hale":

We're out of stock at the moment on #3984-23, but we'll be glad to substitute #4398-41 if you can use them.

I believe I have the qualifications for the position of Assistant Sales Manager advertised in today's *Chronicle*.

Your term life insurance policy No. 23983 will expire June 10 of this year unless you pay premiums of $245 for the past five months.

My Shell Oil Co. credit card No. 987236 has been lost or stolen and I am requesting an immediate replacement.

Will you kindly send me a desk copy of M. L. Stein's *Reporting Today: The Newswriter's Handbook,* which I have assigned to my Beginning Reporting class?

I have not received delivery of a bedroom suite purchased at your store on April 4, six weeks ago.

Will you please send me a bulletin, admission forms and other information about your university and its chemistry department?

Clarity and Conciseness

Many business letters are so shrouded in rhetorical fog that they leave the reader gasping in astonishment. Their point — if they have one — is not made clear. Usually, the writer has resorted to obscure language, vague generalizations or shaded meanings. For some reason, he won't come right out and say what he means. If a letter is to accomplish its objective, it must be understandable. The message must be clear if some kind of answer or reaction is expected. Here is an example of a muddled letter:

Dear Mr. Long:

In going through our files we have discovered that you have been remiss concerning your obligations to maintain communication with this firm concerning the disposal of your late uncle's property in Alton County. As a result, we have deemed it necessary to withdraw our previous offer to act as your representative in attempting to effect a disposition of said property to those interested and qualified as purchasers.

We are unable to determine at this time if said property is suitable in terms of the present real estate market, pending communication with you on its availability and approximate value, according to your position.

Compare that mass of verbage to this letter:

Dear Mr. Hamilton:

Would your firm be interested in selling a tire that provides fifty percent more tread-life than today's standard one, twelve percent more gas mileage, quicker steering response and better traction on wet, icy and snowy roads?

We can supply you with such a tire, and at a competitive price. It is tomorrow's tire today!

But don't take my word alone. Our sales rep, Dawson Taylor, will call on you about December 3 with samples and test results. Mr. Taylor will phone you a week ahead for an appointment.

When you see the tire, I think you'll agree that it is the most exciting transportation breakthrough in ten years.

One way to insure clear, tight writing is to weed out trite, old-fashioned phrases that interfere with communication. These include:

I am pleased to inform you . . .

Your interest in our endeavor is most appreciated.

Please advise me if we can be of further service.

Thanking you in advance . . .

I'm sure you will be pleased to know . . .

In reference to your recent inquiry . . .

Instead of these tired phrases, why not get directly to the point. Rather than "I am pleased to inform you . . . ," say "We found your missing order and are shipping it out today."

Job hunters also hurt their chances by failing the conciseness test. An employer is primarily interested in the applicant's qualifications for the job. He doesn't want to read the person's entire history from the day he was born. Yet, numerous job-seeking letters are loaded with this unnecessary information. They are long, rambling narratives, burdened with irrelevant material, sometimes including the applicant's marital problems, early fears and current hardships.

On the other hand, it's not wise to come on too strong. Letters that begin, "Look no further, I'm the man you want!" rarely make the grade. Whatever comes after that opening had better be outstanding if the writer is to stand a chance. It's better to take a more modest approach while delivering the goods.

Clarity and conciseness also will come easier if you know what you want to say in the letter. Think over your objective before you write. What do you hope to accomplish? What is the problem? If you have everything sorted out in your mind, the letter may require only three paragraphs instead of the eight or nine to which you may be prone. Highway signs are as good a model as any for concise letter writing. They say simply, "Left Turn," "No U Turn," "Slippery When Wet," "Keep Right" and "Yield." The driver registers the message in a split second. Considering the heavy load of business correspondence borne by many companies, it would seem that lean, taut writing should have a high priority.

Empathy

But there's more to business writing than brevity and clearness. There's also empathy — the art of putting yourself in another's place. Successful correspondence often depends on making the recipient feel that he is really understood, that the writer can relate to his problems. This gives what could be a cold, neutral communication warmth and generosity.

The use of *we* and *you* is important in letters seeking to create empathy. Rather than sound like a "soulless" corporation, the sender refers to his firm as "we" and to the receiver as "you." If an enraged customer has complained bitterly about the fact that his $600 couch is falling apart after three weeks of use, something more than a formal acknowledgment is necessary if the store wants to retain his business. The answer might go like this:

Dear Mrs. Lathrop:

   We are truly sorry about the problem with your couch. I'm aware of the inconvenience and embarrassment this must have caused you.
   The workmanship of Mastercraft Furniture is normally of the highest quality. You can be sure that we shall make every effort to discover the cause of the damage and give you full satisfaction if warranted. Mr. James Lowery of our Customer Relations Department will get in touch with you within 48 hours on the matter.

   Even in letters containing bad news, a little empathy will go a long way. If someone has lost out in competing for a job, made an error, or directed his letter to the wrong person or department, you can respond in a way that will not make him feel inferior or stupid. The applicant can be told that his qualifications were excellent but that the position drew a number of highly qualified aspirants. To someone who has made a mistake, the reply could note that anyone might have gone awry on the matter. The postage is the same for such a letter and the gain in goodwill may be enormous.

   Watch out for words that may irritate a correspondent — or even lose him as a customer. Let's assume an appliance dealer in Ohio writes to a supplier in Detroit, inquiring about a delayed shipment of stoves. The stove company's distributing executive replies:

   Your complaint of June 29 has been received and is being referred to the appropriate department. Please advise me if there is anything else I can do for you.

   This letter is not only cold but the wording is awful. The dealer may not have meant his message as a complaint at all. He will probably resent having it labeled as such. A more adroit response would be:

> I very much regret that your order has not been filled on schedule. I've taken immediate action on the matter and you should receive the shipment shortly. If it hasn't arrived in a week, please call me collect.

The idea in business letters is to keep customers, not lose them. The tone of a letter can make the difference.

When replying to a hostile letter, cool off for a day or two before answering. It's not necessary to match the person's rudeness or arrogance. You have to consider your reputation and that of your firm. Replying in kind puts you on the other's level.

It's also a wise idea to keep jokes, political comments, and personality references out of correspondence. Such insertions can backfire.

Persuasion

The object of many business letters is to persuade someone to do something, whether it's to buy, to sell, to cease and desist, to change his mind or to apply or supply information. The language used will often determine the success of the correspondence.

Facts are the main persuader. Soft-soaping won't help if the arguments lack force and credibility. If you're offering someone a bargain, it has to be spelled out. "The best magazine that money can buy" is a bit of self-idolatry that means little without supporting statements. What *is* likely to arouse the reader is the promise of a year's subscription at $5.25, "$2.00 less than the regular price." That's a fact that can be readily digested.

Money isn't the only means of making a persuasive appeal. Other motives include ambition, love, health, personal appearance, cooperation, competition, personal development, curiosity, education, safety, popularity, reputation, opportunity and good citizenship.

In each case, however, the evidence must be present. You must *show* an individual how your course of instruction will aid his personal development. If there is a valid opportunity, it must be convincing enough to overcome natural skepticism at offers of this nature. Many people believe the old adage "There is no such thing as a free lunch."

Persuasion, then, is a matter of winning confidence. If the reader believes in you, your task is accomplished. If he doesn't, you've failed. The difference lies in the soundness of your argument or explanation. Never underestimate the reader's intelligence. Even the most unsophisticated individual has one key attribute going for him: common sense. This is the barrier you must hurdle.

Exercises

1. An appliance company has refused to honor the warranty on your color television set, which doesn't work. Write a complaint letter to the firm's sales manager, telling him the problem in precise terms.

2. Ask a local company if you may have copies of ten or fifteen of their recent business letters. Read them carefully, to determine if they can be improved by using clearer language, tighter phrasing, etc.

3. Your library should have books on writing business letters. Read one or two, paying particular attention to the good and bad examples.

CHAPTER ELEVEN

Writing for Money

There are only about 250 men and women in the United States who make their living entirely from free-lance writing. They are tops in their field, with incomes ranging from $20,000 to $100,00 a year. Much of their work is done on assignment from magazine editors, book publishers or television and movie producers.

But don't let these facts discourage you. Hundreds of other people are part-time free-lancers. They include housewives, teachers, cab drivers, newspaper reporters, secretaries, social workers and prison inmates. Some are determined to be full-time writers; others are content to sell an occasional magazine article while making a living at another occupation. Consider, also, that the 250 writers mentioned above will not be the same 250 names five or ten years from now. Some will be replaced by newcomers who are unknown today.

Basic Equipment

Mastery of the English language is essential for professional writing. If you think that editors will take care of your bad grammar and syntax, you're in for a shock. Manuscripts that don't meet English requirements are rejected. Variations in style are permitted — even welcomed — but there's not much a publisher can do with an article or story that fails the English test.

Grammatical competence isn't enough, however. The writer must also have a sense of style — a way of putting words together so they will attract and hold readers. This knack can be developed through constant practice and by reading and studying the styles of established authors. The effective writer states his ideas clearly, using language the reader understands.

The Writer's Makeup

Whatever else writing is, it also is a state of mind. To be a professional writer, you must be prepared to give up some comforts, pleasures and even association with your family and friends. You must stay at your typewriter several hours a day without distractions. One well-known author won't even answer telephone calls while working. Another won't have a phone in his study.

Your writing room should be out of the mainstream of family life, even if you have to board up a section of the basement. A writer's output varies but few professionals depend on inspiration. Some writers set a daily quota for themselves — perhaps two or three thousand words. Others view their task like a regular job, forcing themselves to remain at the typewriter for six or eight hours a day. Some write in the morning and take the afternoon off. Still others can only work late at night or in the early morning.

The point is that you should place yourself under some kind of discipline if you hope to see your name in print. Find a schedule that is best for you and stick to it. Nothing gets written simply by thinking or talking about it. *You must work!*

And that isn't all. You must *keep working* in the face of discouraging results. For unless you are unusual, you will get rejection notices. Patience and determination are considered old-fashioned virtues but no one needs them more than a writer. It's hard to face a typewriter the same day a manuscript has come back to you, but that's exactly what you must do if you hope to become published. You may take heart from the fact that one woman writer sent her manuscript out thirty times before a magazine bought it. Another writer labored for three years before he sold an article. Both are now among the most successful writers in the country.

Preparing Manuscripts

It's important that your copy have a professional look. It should be typewritten double-spaced on standard-size white paper. Your name, address and telephone number go in the upper left corner. The word count is placed in the upper right corner, along with the rights you are offering for sale, e.g., North American, all, etc. The title appears a third of the way down the page and underneath it your by-line, which may or may not be the same as the name in the left corner. Be sure to number each page and put your name on them as well. Manuscripts sometimes get lost or separated in publishers' offices. Most editors want a manuscript to be accompanied by a self-addressed stamped envelope. To keep your script in good condition, it's a good idea to place cardboard backing in the envelope. By the way, any story or article over three pages should be sent unfolded in a large, manila envelope.

A writer should keep track of what he has in the mail as well as sales, rejections and expenses. Three-by-five index cards or a loose-leaf notebook are fine for this purpose. Remember, legitimate expenses in connection with your writing such as postage, paper, typewriter ribbons and traveling are deductible on your income tax provided you can show income from writing. Hold on to your receipts.

The Query

Professional writers usually query magazine editors on articles. The query can be a one-page, single-spaced letter that describes your idea in a provocative way. The purpose is to arouse the editor's interest to the point where he will invite you to submit the whole piece. The first paragraph of your letter can be the same as the one you use in the finished article.

An editor's favorable reaction to a query is not a promise to buy the article, but it's nevertheless a bright sign for you. It means he thinks enough of the idea to want to see a completed manuscript. What he doesn't know — particularly if you are a new writer — is whether you can write the article to meet his publication's standards. If not, he can reject it, whatever his response to your query. Still, getting a green light on a query is far better than sending your manuscript in "over the transom," as they say in editorial offices. First, it signifies that you are acting like a professional. Second, the article is virtually certain to get a careful reading. Finally, it saves you a lot of needless work. Writing on speculation is a risky business, especially if you are unfamiliar with an editor's needs and desires. When your query excites curiosity, you at least know that the welcome mat will be out for your manuscript.

Here is a typical query letter:

Mr. Stanley Green, Managing Editor
L.I. Magazine
Newsday
Garden City, N.Y.

Dear Mr. Green:

On a June day in 1965, Francis J. Duane, a busy and vigorous golf course architect, had trouble climbing the stairs to his second-floor office in Port Washington, N.Y. Within 24 hours he was completely paralyzed from the neck down in what was the beginning of an ordeal that took him to the brink of death.

Today, Frank Duane, working from a wheelchair, is one of the top golf course architects in the U.S., flying 80,000 to 100,000 miles a year to create some of the poshest fairways in the country. His talents have been employed at Sea Pines Plantation, Hilton Head, S.C.; Chet Huntley's Big Sky resort in Montana; the Mariner Sands Country Club, Stuart, Fla.; Marshwood and Sidaway Island, Ga. and a number of others.

Duane's story involves great personal courage, a large and loving family who stood by him and a unique talent. He creates courses for the Sunday duffer as well as the champions who have praised his work.

I feel the story would interest both the golf enthusiasts and readers attracted to the "triumph-over-disaster" account. I have several anecdotes that would make it a warmly human narrative of universal appeal.

Please advise me as soon as possible if you are interested.

Yours sincerely,

Before you put an idea into query form, check to see if it's been used before and, if so, how recently. *The Reader's Guide to Periodical Literature* is one source for checking, although it doesn't list all magazines. Above all, scan back issues of the publication at which you're aiming to see if it has carried a piece about your subject. This can save you embarrassment later.

Know Your Market

Many writers fail to sell their material because they haven't researched their market. They submit articles to magazines with little or no idea of what these periodicals use. If you want to crack the *New Yorker*, for example, you should familiarize yourself with its contents, including the advertising. This will tell you that the magazine aims for a sophisticated readership that is, for the most part, well educated and in the higher income bracket. A search through *Harper's, Atlantic Monthly* and *New Republic* would reveal articles dealing with politics, social change and education. The so-called men's magazines such as *Esquire, Playboy, Argosy* and *True* have particular requirements to which the writer must pay attention. The same is true of women's publications, although their content has changed drastically in recent years. A number of these periodicals accept articles on controversial topics if they're well written and documented.

An editor has only to glance at a page or two of a manuscript to know whether the author is acquainted with his magazine. Spare yourself his irritation (and rejection) by reading thoroughly the publications for which you are writing. You might also get a copy of *Writer's Market,* published by Writer's Digest of Cincinnati, Ohio. The *Market* is a yearbook containing the names and descriptions of nearly five thousands paying markets for novels, stories, fillers, plays, articles, gags, verse and photos.

Today's writing market calls for much more nonfiction than fiction. There's a dwindling demand for the latter which is primarily met by established authors. If you leaf through general circulation and women's magazines, you will note that nonfiction articles predominate heavily. The popularity of television is said to account in part for the minor place of stories in periodicals. Nonetheless, a few major magazines such as *Atlantic, New Yorker,* and *Harper's* feature high-quality fiction.

What Sells

Writing begins with an idea. Ideas sell stories and articles. A magazine editor is likely to give a go-ahead on a query because of the central idea. He is hooked on its novelty or originality. Magazine articles these days must present a fresh viewpoint and approach. Publications that deal in topical content don't want long-winded opinion pieces or historical essays. The editor of a travel magazine isn't looking for another article telling all the standard places to see in Paris or London. Such pieces have been done hundreds of times before. He will, however, consider an article about an out-of-the-way French village noted for its wineries or a quaint, little-known street in London where shops specialize in antique silver. A woman's magazine has no room for flatly written articles extolling motherhood, but it will be receptive to one about a mother's role in the women's liberation movement.

Ideas can come from various sources. Many professional writers browse through three or four newspapers a day, seeking items that could be turned into articles — or even books. Ideas also may emerge from your work, friends or simple observation. The ability to spot trends and developments is important to the nonfiction writer. Carry a small notebook with you at all times and jot down ideas that occur to you. A vacation trip or any new experience may lead to a nice check from a publisher. It's happened more than once.

If you're serious about free-lance writing, start keeping an idea file. Tuck away ideas you may find in newspaper clippings, the classroom, conversations with friends, TV and radio broadcasts, etc. The arrangement of your file doesn't matter if *you* know where everything is. Keep adding to each idea. One day you may find that you have enough for a full-length magazine article — or even a book. Look for the odd, the unique, the offbeat, the new, the topical. When you read a newspaper item, ask yourself: did it say everything about the subject a reader might want to know? If not, there may be a magazine piece to be developed. Be curious. Look for facts *not* given in the news story. That is, look elsewhere.

The Magazine Market Picture

General circulation magazines have been declining while specialized periodicals are enjoying a boom. In recent years, such well-known publications as *Life*, the weekly *Saturday Evening Post, Look, This Week* and *Woman's Home Companion* have folded. But meanwhile scores of special interest magazines have sprung up; most of them are markets for the free-lancer. The subjects include sports, women's liberation, astrology, music, travel and leisure, religion, hobbies, black personalities and affairs, popularized science and health.

Even so, it's unwise for the beginner to specialize too narrowly. For one thing, most of these magazines pay modest fees, some as low as $25. Then, too, why limit yourself when there are so many markets available? Despite the attrition, there are still several high-paying general consumer magazines alive. The *Reader's Digest*, to cite one example, offers as much as $2,500 for an original article; some of the articles it publishes have been written by neophytes.

One group that should not be overlooked is the trade and industrial magazines. These magazines perhaps lack the glamour of the others, but they are a steady market for free-lancers. There are hundreds of them, covering such areas as agriculture, business, education, supermarkets, hardware, jewelry, florists, construction, home furnishings, pharmacy, photography, textiles, real estate, etc. Editors of these publications want articles, features and fillers that will be of economic benefit to their readers. A subscriber to a magazine on hospitals and nursing homes would read with great interest an article on a new, disposable surgical gown. A florist would be intrigued by an account of a flower shop owner in another state who developed a system for speeding up deliveries. In other words, the writer for these magazines must have a strong slant to his articles. A list of these publications can be found in *Writer's Market* and other market guides.

Here for example, is a description of the free-lance requirements of *Shopping Center World*, a magazine for real estate developers and investors, as reported in *Writer's Market:*

> How to articles on specific centers or subjects — cutting costs of construction, promoting a center, increasing its cash flow, selecting a site, etc.

Or take this one from *Hospital Physician:*

> Occasionally buys "penetrating articles that reflect the vitality and ferment in medicine today. Also fast-moving, helpful articles giving practical advice on socio-economic aspects of a young doctor's life and education. Possible subjects could be training, pay, workload, diagnosis, clinical developments, medico-legal problems, career guidance; personal relationships with patients, the public, students; savings, investment, family life, establishing private practice."

Remember, in magazines like these, you're writing for a specialized audience and you must keep their interests in mind.

Books

The author of a magazine article or story is paid a flat sum of money for which he usually surrenders rights to the work. A book author, in contrast, is given an advance on royalties if the book is accepted. If the advance is, say, $2,500, the publisher deducts this amount from any royalties. From then on, the author is entitled to collect royalties as specified in his contract.

Selling a first book is a tough job. Here are a few tips which might make it easier:

1. It's rare when a first-time author sells a book with a query letter. Publishers usually demand at least an outline and up to three finished chapters.

This is sometimes true of novels as well as non-fiction.

2. As with magazine articles, ideas for nonfiction books must be timely, topical or controversial. Sometimes a magazine article can be expanded into a book. Alvin Toffler's best-selling *Future Shock* is an example.

3. Manuscripts should be neatly typewritten. If you can't do it, hire a professional typist. Always keep at least one copy yourself.

4. It's considered bad form to send an outline or completed manuscript to more than one publisher at a time.

5. For the actual writing, set up some kind of schedule for yourself or the book will never get done. The average novel is about sixty thousand words. Many nonfiction books go well over that. You can see that you have your work cut out for you.

Should You Have an Agent?

If your writing base is Rolla, Missouri, a New York literary agent can be a big help. But there's a catch. Reputable agents are reluctant to handle unpublished writers. They're businessmen and businesswomen who work on a ten percent commission of their client's earnings. So, of course, they prefer dealing with established authors.

Be wary of advertisements in which agents ask for a "reading fee." Some of these persons are legitimate agents who deal mostly with new writers. Others, however, are shady operators who perform little or no service for the fee. The better-known agents do not charge a reading fee.

If you haven't published, you may obtain the services of a reputable representative through the recommendation of an established author. And there's always the chance that your unsolicited manuscript might impress an agent so much that he's willing to take a chance on you. After all, literary agents, like other businessmen, must think of the future. They look for promising writers.

Agents spare you the chore of sending a manuscript to publisher after publisher. They know the market thoroughly, which means your manuscript is not subjected to a fishing expedition. A final note: It's just about impossible to sell movie and television scripts without an agent. Buyers simply won't handle them directly from the author.

Selling Pictures

If you're a good enough photographer to illustrate your own articles, you can make extra free-lance money. Most magazines pay an additional amount for photos. In some instances, publications will use staff photographers for assignments or hire a free-lance cameraman. But let's say you have the responsibility for photos. If you find a professional photographer to work with you, advise him to make his own financial arrangements with the magazine. This gets you out of the delicate middleman role in establishing his fee.

Keep in mind that "handout" or free pictures are available in connection with many articles. If you are doing a personality profile of a prominent tycoon or entertainer, his public relations staff is certain to have art. Another photo source is the local newspaper, but you'll probably have to pay.

Some travel magazines favor authors who can provide their own illustrations of an article. If you are serious about being a nonfiction writer, it won't hurt to invest in a good camera and learn how to use it.

A Final Word

This is probably not the first book on writing you have read. And perhaps it won't be the last.

That's fine, but keep one fact in mind: reading about writing is not enough. You've also got to write. Those who achieve any fluency as writers keep at it. Any skill becomes rusty with disuse.

You may want to try your hand at free-lance writing. This certainly is one good way to develop your skill and talent.

But it isn't the only way. If you're a student, look for courses that demand writing assignments: term papers, essays, reports, etc. Many students try to avoid these classes and they suffer for it. By the time they graduate, their writing proficiency is so poor that they have trouble qualifying for jobs that require communication ability. As one prominent journalist recently put it: "College students don't learn to write and about the only thing they read are T-shirts."

If you are in the business or professional world, find excuses to write reports, memos, letters, evalutions, etc. Work on polishing your style, keeping in mind the principles laid out in this book. If you don't think that you can properly critique your efforts, seek out competent professionals who can help you. One self-aid is to compare what you write today with what you wrote last year or five years ago. Do you notice any improvement? Are your sentences shorter, crisper, clearer? Are you getting to the point more quickly? Is there a smoother transition from sentence to sentence and from paragraph to paragraph? Is the fat trimmed off?

If you're not in a position to write as a student or job holder, pump out letters to friends, relatives and the editor of your local newspaper. Or you may want to put your thoughts on paper — whether they are about the state of the economy or the book you just read. Who knows? You may be able to interest a newspaper or magazine in publishing your book review. More than one idle thought — put on paper — has found its way into print. In any event, keep writing!

One learns to write by writing.

And by reading. In my writing classes, I have found that the top students are fairly heavy readers of newspapers, magazines and books. They consciously or unconsciously have absorbed a sense of style. Their writing may be imitative at first, but this is true of most writers.

The important element is that they come to class with a feeling for words.

If you don't already, subscribe to at least one newspaper, and two or three magazines. Join a book club.

Newspapers and periodicals are available in your library, but there's something about having reading matter in the home that prompts one to read. By all means, make use of your library as a source for additional reading. How many books did you read last year? If you didn't read at least eight, you missed a great opportunity to improve your writing skill. Do you read a newspaper every day? You should.

And read for style as well as content. Notice how professional writers put words together to form ideas. Learn from them.

The ability to write well is one of the greatest treasures you can possess.

Develop it.

ACKNOWLEDGMENTS

AP Newsfeatures

for excerpt from a newspaper article datelined Washington.

The Boston Globe

for a review of the musical "Shenandoah," by *Boston Globe* reporter Kevin Kelly.

Clipper

for excerpt from the article "Can We Save The World's Treasures?," by Beverly Ann Deepe. Copyright © 1972 by Pan American World Airways, Inc.

Gordon Davidson

Artistic Director of the Center Theater Group at the Mark Taper Forum, Los Angeles, California for an excerpt from an article appearing in the *Los Angeles Times*.

Harvard Lampoon

for an article from the Cosmopolitan Magazine Parody, 1972.

Barbara Moore Lee

for the term paper "An American Eve."

Los Angeles Times

for excerpt from the editorial "Setting-a-Poor-Example Dept.," *Los Angeles Times*, January 14, 1975. Copyright © 1975 by *Los Angeles Times*. Reprinted by permission.

NOTES

NOTES

NOTES

NOTES

NOTES

NOTES

NOTES

NOTES